6-26-95

Ray + Ariel —
Be good to each
other & continue
to love —
Peace
Stu

TWICE BLESSED

TWICE BLESSED

Art Metrano laughs the darkness away

ART METRANO WITH CYNTHIA LEE

WRS
PUBLISHING

A Division of WRS Group, Inc.
Waco, Texas

First published in the United States of America in 1995 by WRS Publishing, A division of WRS Group, Inc., 701 N. New Road, Waco, Texas 76710
Book design by Kenneth Turbeville
Jacket design by Joe James

10 9 8 7 6 5 4 3 2 1

Library of Congress Cataloging-in-Publication Data

Metrano, Art.
    Twice blessed : Art Metrano laughs the darkness away / Art Metrano, Cynthia Lee.
        p.   cm.
    ISBN 1-56796-060-X : $19.95
    1. Metrano, Art. 2. Spinal cord--Wounds and injuries--Patients-
-Biography. 3. Actors--United States--Biography. I. Lee, Cynthia
II. Title.
RD796.M48A3   1995
362.1'97482'0092--dc20
    [B]   94-32720
                                                              CIP

DEDICATION

For my wife, Becky, whose strength and love have taught me how to live life one day at a time... to share my feelings openly and honestly and acknowledge those who love me. I love you.

For my mother, Becky, and my brother, Ben: you both have taught me how to laugh out loud, love with all my heart, and live life to the fullest.

For Roxanne, my eldest daughter, for being there when I needed you most... I love you.

For Harry and Zoë, for all the hugs and kisses, for falling asleep in my arms, for keeping me young, for making me laugh. For never seeing my disability. For taking me to another level... I love you.

For Rhonda Braha. You came every morning and fed me breakfast, emptied my urinal, checked my chart, helped my wife, watched the kids, and threw away my sleeping pills... I will be forever grateful.

TABLE OF CONTENTS

ACKNOWLEDGMENTS

Bill Birnes, you have opened the door for me. You're a terrific guy and a very smart agent. Thank you for finding the right publisher for this book. The work is now completed. There will be no more emergency phone calls, I hope.

For all my friends who came to the hospital, brought me food, rubbed my feet, got my name in the paper, told me jokes, sent flowers, cooked me pasta, made me laugh, took me on midnight wheelchair journeys through Cedars-Sinai, I thank you all: Harvey Fisher, Robert Dunlap, Sandy Sirkus, Felice Orlandi, Jed and Toby Allen, Bernie Katz, Lou Alexander, Erik Estrada, Joe Bologna, Dan Paulson, Rodney Sheldon, Mimi Weber, Carol Connors, David and Nancy Zelon, Andy Chute, Earl Finn, Mark Miller, Richard Faun, Jack Carter, Norm Crosby, Jerry Vale, Ellyn Stern, Lavelle Roby, Mike Robelo, Vivian and Marty Kove, Jim Green, Rudy DeLuca, James De Yarman, Dennis Cole, Creative Arts Temple, Sid Young, Barbara Bingham, Billy Brown, Owen Francis, Anne and Bill Katzky, Rabbi Jerry Cutler, Rabbi Robert Gan, Francine Aron, Marty Abrams, David and Romi Goldsmith, Ken Amorasano, Dr. Dudley Danoff, Allan Epstein, Madlyn Rhue, R.G. Armstrong, Richard Kaufman, Larry Spiegal, Irwin and Jane Russo, Artie Butler, Daryl Belisle, Joel Chernoff, Dan Chasin, Sally Marr, Steve Silberfein, and Dr. Max Lerman.

Thank you to my sisters Lilly and Shirley for coming out from New York and helping me and my family, and to my son, Howard, for your love and understanding.

I also want to acknowledge the many friends and associates who helped launch my play, *Twice Blessed*, upon which this book is based: Paul Maslansky for seeing the possibility and making it happen; Tony

Thomas and Bill Cunningham, who came to the backers' audition and said, "We want to help," and did; Sanford Gage for his friendship and legal advice; Craig T. Nelson and Barry Levinson for their friendship and love; David Sheehan and Bob Berger for your support; Dr. Jerry Buss for always being there for me and my family; Mark Travis for your input in directing the first production of the play; George Dzundza for taking the play to another level; Rod Lathim and Access Theater for believing in the play and giving it a first-class production. See you all opening night in New York.

God bless, to you all!

RONALD REAGAN
October 5, 1989

Dear Art:

Just a quick note to say how sorry Nancy and I are to learn of your hospitalization. Please know that our thoughts and prayers are with you as you are faced with this difficult personal challenge. We hope that you will find great strength and comfort in the loving care of family and friends -- there's no better medicine!

With our very best wishes and God bless you.

Sincerely,

Ronald Reagan

Mr. Art Metrano
Cedar-Sinai Medical Center
Schuman Building, Room 841
8700 Beverly Boulevard
Los Angeles, California 90048

FOREWORD

Art Metrano and I are from Brooklyn, where there remains today something like a brotherhood among those of us who grew up and went to school together in the forties and fifties. We reconnect at high school reunions, weddings, funerals—that sort of gathering of people who have forged a common bond. It was the place that formed us, the place that we left behind to become who we are today, and yet the place that will always be a part of who we are.

Like me, Art has a strong sense of his beginnings. And when it came time for Life to smack him in the face and leave him for dead, he looked inward (and backward) at those people and at those places to find the strength to deal with what had happened to him.

At times in our lives (and we will all have such times if we live long enough), we must make an assessment of the ruins of our situation and decide, as Art did, if we want to continue or to give up and quit. If we do want to live, then we have to figure out how to do it. If we're wise and courageous, we learn from the pain. After we figure out that God won't pull any puppet strings and make things right for us, we learn those life lessons that we would never have had an opportunity to learn if it weren't for the pain. Valuable lessons. Priceless lessons.

My "moment of truth" was my heart attack. Your moment of truth will be something else. These very hardest of life's rows to hoe have a way of calling our attention to where we've been and where we're going. And when all is said and done, we know we've come a long way when we can finally say, "I am a better man because of it."

No one who knows him would deny that Art was down and almost out—for a while. And yet, he has come back, a long way back—in his own words, a better man. He wants us to know him, and he wants to teach us something of the important things of life—lessons of hope, lessons of forgiveness, lessons of love.

Way to go, Art!

—Larry King
Host of CNN's "Larry King Live!"

P.S.: The only thing better than reading this book is seeing the play by the same name. Readers, if you ever get a chance to see Art in *Twice Blessed* in New York or Los Angeles or wherever, don't let the opportunity slip by.

The quality of mercy is not strain'd,—

It droppeth as the gentle rain from heaven

Upon the place beneath: it is twice bless'd,—

It blesseth him that gives, and him that takes:

It is an attribute to God himself...

The Merchant of Venice
—William Shakespeare
Portia's speech
Act IV, Scene I

CHAPTER ONE

THE HANGMAN'S BREAK

As I stepped up the extension part of the ladder, I felt it give way. I knew something awful was about to happen, but there was no stopping it. All I'd wanted to do was hose off the balcony, but it was not meant to be. Suddenly I was falling backward toward the ground, hurtling through the air as fast as the speed of light, or so it seemed. That was on Sunday, September 17, 1989—the day my life was turned upside down.

It was a beautiful Sunday morning, one of those rare days in Los Angeles when you can actually see the skyline. The brown haze that usually hangs over the city had disappeared for the weekend. No smog! It was not a typical LA day, if you know what I mean—"I shot an arrow in the air and it stuck!" to paraphrase Shakespeare.

But on this particular day, the sky was so blue it was almost translucent. There wasn't a cloud in sight. I remember admiring the spectacular sweep of the Hollywood hills as I drove along Sunset Boulevard. Tall, elegant palm trees swayed gently in the breeze. On days like this, I understand why LA is called the City of Angels.

I had just finished playing tennis doubles with friends. I'd had a good game and felt terrific, really on top of the world. My wife and I had recently purchased a second home that we were renovating and had put up for sale. I was driving over to take a look at the new pool we were having built.

As I drove up to the house, my mind was racing forward through the day. At one o'clock, the real estate broker had prospective buyers coming to see the house. At three, I would meet my wife, Becky, and our two children at Roxbury Park. We'd planned to have dinner in Chinatown and then see a movie. The following morning, I had an audition for a part in a new film. My life was everything I wanted it to be. I was feeling powerful, in charge of my own destiny.

I pulled my '82 Corvette up to the garage door, got out, and entered through the front gate. Taking two steps at a time, I went down the stairs at the side of the house which led to the backyard pool and spa. What I encountered once I got there was an eyesore. Over the past eight months, the house had been completely renovated, inside an out, but the pool and spa were still not finished. The backyard was strewn with debris left by workmen, and mounds of dirt were everywhere.

As I looked around in disgust, I notice that gray cement spray was all over the back walls, windows, and doors. It was gunite spray from the pool. I didn't want potential buyers of the house to see the mess, so I got a hose and began to wash it off. Because the balcony was also covered with gunite, I grabbed a ladder and set it firmly against the balcony. I knew that a home buyer would want to step out onto the balcony to see the view. Then he'd end up tracking the gunite spray back into the house and onto the new white berber carpet I had had installed.

But all my plans to clean up the mess evaporated into thin air as I went flying to the ground like a kamikaze pilot. I don't have the words to describe the terror of that moment. There wasn't time to think, let alone figure out a way to cushion my fall.

I hit the ground head first. I heard a snap in my neck. I tried to move, but couldn't. I watched my right hand curl up. I couldn't feel anything. My entire body was limp. I tried to scream for help, but I had no voice. My tongue was stuck in the back of my throat and I was having trouble breathing. And then a terrible realization hit me—I had no sensation in my arms and legs! I tried like hell not to panic.

As I lay there, the sun was blinding. I closed my eyes to escape the glare. The minute I did, I saw a guy falling off a ladder. The top of his head hits the ground. He gets up... walks away... stops... turns around and looks back at me, then smiles. I thought my mind was playing tricks on me. Everything was in black and white, like a '50s horror movie.

I opened my eyes again, but glare from the sun was like a laser beam, so I closed them again. And then I saw the same scene over again. A guy falls off a ladder, the top of his head hits the ground, he gets up, walks away, stops, and smiles back at me. I kept saying to myself, Who is that? I don't recognize him. It's not me, is it?

I wondered what the hell was going on. My breathing became more difficult. I felt as if there were a ton of bricks on my chest, and I was terrified I was dying. I closed my eyes again, and I saw the same guy falling off the ladder, repeating the same sequence of events. I thought I was having an out-of-body experience and my spirit was leaving my body for good. Please God, I don't want to die. I decided I wasn't going to close my eyes again no matter what!

I began to think that maybe I was dreaming. Maybe the whole thing was just a horrible illusion and I'd wake up, have lunch with my wife and kids, and I'd be able to walk again. But try as I might, I still couldn't move a muscle. I knew then it was no dream.

As I lay there, staring up at the sky, I thought of Roy Campanella—the great baseball player who became a quadriplegic after a near-fatal car accident. I was terrified I'd be like him. That fear made me scream out. But my voice wasn't there. I tried again and again to scream, but my tongue was in the way. It was stuck in the back of my throat and my breathing was getting worse.

I don't know how I found the strength to keep trying to call out, but I wouldn't give up. Finally, I got the words out of my mouth.

"Somebody help me!"

I heard myself say it, but it didn't sound like me. I tried again.

"Somebody... please, help me!"

My voice was unrecognizable to me. It sounded like I had too much food crammed in my mouth. My voice was garbled and I was incapable of sounding out the words properly. It was as if I were deaf and didn't know how to speak. The more I tried to mouth the words that might get me some help, the more I realized that panic was really setting in. I screamed out again in my garbled voice.

"God, will somebody please help me!"

But no one was around. It was a quiet Sunday morning and I was all alone. How the hell had I done this to myself? I assured myself that I would be all right, that someone would walk by and call an ambulance. But what if no one saw me? I couldn't yell loudly enough to get attention. Maybe I'd have to lie here all damn day.

Suddenly, it occurred to me that the real estate broker would be here at one with prospective buyers. It was an open house. People would walk through the house and eventually they would come to the yard and they would see me lying there.

I'd look up and I'd say... "Hi, I'm the owner. I just broke my neck, but not to worry. House looks great, eh? Nice gourmet kitchen! And how do you like the two bidets in the master suite? Nice touch, huh?"

I tried to make myself relax, believing I'd be rescued if I could just hold on. I kept going back and forth from hope to despair as the minutes ticked away. I knew with an injury like mine, time was of the essence.

Whatever the damage was it would have to be attended to right away or it might get worse. I kept trying to yell, but I just couldn't make my voice very loud.

An hour went by. The longest hour I've ever lived. Pain was radiating through my right shoulder and I didn't think I could take it anymore. I have never felt more helpless in my life. I began to have an internal, one-way conversation with God. I asked God to help. I begged. And then I pleaded.

"God, did I piss you off? Are you mad at me for something?"

I wanted to make a deal. I promised I'd stop all my bad habits if I could just get up and walk away from this terror. I told God I'd change my anal-compulsive ways. I'd stop trying to have things my way all the time. I'd stop being the asshole I sometimes was. I'd love my wife more. I'd spend more time with my kids.

"Please, God," I implored, "just give me another chance. I don't want to be a cripple."

But if God was listening, God wasn't talking back. I cried out again.

"Please, somebody help me!"

Suddenly, I heard my next door neighbor's dogs barking. They're schnauzers named Adolph and Eva. Then I heard a woman's voice, calling to me over the fence.

"Art, is that you?"

"Yes. Please help me! I fell... I'm paralyzed!"

"Okay, Art, take it easy! I'll call 911. Don't move!"

Don't move? I thought, good idea, I'll stay right where I am!

One of the things that's gotten me through the worst situations in my life has been my sense of humor. I love to tell jokes, to make people laugh. I think my sense of humor has saved me from the hell of depression plenty of times during my life. So when my neighbor told me not to move, I was glad I was able to take her advice with a smile.

From a distance, I heard the wailing sound of an ambulance. I prayed it was coming for me. I shut my eyes and tried to actually will that ambulance into my driveway. The high-pitched squeal of the siren got closer and closer. Like most people, I get a chill down my spine when an ambulance rushes through traffic on its way to rescue someone. It conjures up images of pain and death. But this time, the wailing of the siren was the most beautiful sound I'd ever heard. Now, every time I see an ambulance rushing down the street I say thank you, guys!

I couldn't see the paramedics at first because I was flat on my back. But I heard them coming down the hill and into my yard. One of them yelled out.

"He's a big guy. We're gonna need more help!"

I let out an enormous sigh of relief. At last, I said to myself, they've come to help.

The paramedics were fantastic. I've never seen guys act with more professionalism and courtesy. They were quick, gentle, and sure of what they were doing. I thought maybe I'd be all right after all. One of them asked me a bunch of questions—name, age, height, weight. He reassured me with a compassionate look in his eyes. Then he put a brace around my neck.

"Are you allergic to anything?"

"Yeah," I said smiling. "Rap music."

My sense of humor was coming through again, and I could see by the look on his tan, young, smiling face that my joke was appreciated. He injected me with a drug and then slid a wooden stretcher under me. I could hear them Velcro me up in something warm. I felt like I was in a body bag, but I wasn't complaining. I just wanted to be taken care of.

One of the other paramedics leaned over me and asked:

"Are you comfortable?"

"Well, I make a living!"

The paramedics laughed. I felt my eyes roll back in my head. I passed out.

A half-hour later, I woke up in a tunnel screaming. My right arm was over my head pinned against the inside of a cylinder. Where the hell was I?

"Get me out of here... you're hurting me!" I screamed.

"Take it easy," someone said. "We're taking some X-rays. You'll be out of here in a moment."

"I can't stand it! Please, somebody move my arm down!" I began to cry. "Come on, guys! You're hurting me! Move my arm!" I screamed again. I was squeezed in like a sardine in a can.

The technician finally came over and moved my arm to a more comfortable position.

"You'll only be like this for another moment. Hold on."

They continued to take pictures of my body, painfully and carefully adjusting my body as they did. They seemed to have no emotion. They were just doing their jobs. I was just another emergency patient. They had heard it all before. They finally removed me from this horror chamber, placed me on a gurney, and left me out in the hallway. I lost consciousness.

The next thing I remember, I was staring up at the ceiling, looking at a large circular light. I was at Cedars-Sinai Medical Center in Los Angeles, just a few minutes from where I live, in ICU. I still couldn't move, couldn't feel anything. Everything around me seemed blurry. After a few minutes, the room came into focus. There were two doctors leaning over me. One of them was holding a syringe.

"Mister Metrano," he said, "you're gonna feel a little prick to your head."

"But Doctor, we just met!" I said, in a drug-induced euphoria.

He injected a needle into my head, but I felt nothing. I closed my eyes, and I was off in never-never land.

I kept going in and out of consciousness for what seemed like an eternity. Then a strange sound brought me out of the fog. I heard a ratchet wrench very close to my head.

'ed they were putting screws into my skull,
ack. That sound was like someone tightening
.uts on a tire, only the tire was my brain.

I drifted back into unconsciousness. When I woke up, my head was surrounded by a weird contraption that looked like a bird cage. It had four bars and was all around my head.

I felt like I was inside a prison and my skull was attached to it. I had breathing tubes down my throat and up my nose, a tube in my penis, an IV in my arm pumping steroids, and a morphine drip for pain.

As I lay there, I heard my wife, Becky, talking with someone just outside the door.

"Mrs. Metrano, I'm afraid your husband's injury is very serious."

"How serious, Doctor?" Becky asked.

"Depending on how badly the spinal cord is damaged, he may have to spend the rest of his life in an electrical wheelchair. He may even need the help of a ventilator to breathe."

Becky was silent. I wanted to scream at the top of my lungs, but I couldn't move a damn muscle. All I could do was yell and scream inside my head.

There's no way I'm gonna sit in a wheelchair, breathing through a tube the rest of my life! Not me! I'll wheel that damn thing onto the Hollywood freeway and look for a Mack truck.

Of course with my luck, my wheelchair would probably have dual air bags and I'd live through that, too. Thank you, Mr. Iacocca! Did you know that Iacocca stands for I Am Chairman Of the Chrysler Corporation of America?

Then I heard the doctor tell her:

"It looks as if the neck is broken in two places, cervical one and two. They control the respiratory system."

"Is that why he's having trouble breathing?" Becky asked, her voice shaking.

"Yes," the doctor said. "That's what has caused his tongue to go to the back of his throat. He has what we call the 'Hangman's Break.' It's the kind of break that kills people. He's lucky to be alive."

Lucky? I thought. What the hell is that doctor talking about? Luck is when you win the lottery or have a lead in a hit TV series. You call this *lucky*?

But no one could hear me. My thoughts were locked inside a body that couldn't move. I couldn't speak or communicate in any way. I wasn't even in the same world everyone else was in.

This is what hell is all about, I thought. I'm in it. I'm *living* it.

CHAPTER TWO

BEFORE THE FALL

Prior to my accident, I thought I had my life pretty well under control. My acting career was in full tilt and my family life was good. Becky and I had our problems like any couple does, and sometimes the kids were more than a handful, but my life was going the direction I wanted it to go. Or so I thought. Having a near fatal accident can change your perception of life. It can, and should, alter the way you think and act. It can force you to really think about what you are, who you are, and where you came from.

I was born in Brooklyn, New York. The name on my birth certificate reads "Arthur Mesistrano." My father took out the s-i-s because he thought Metrano was easier to pronounce. A lot of people thought we were Italian, but we're Sephardic Jews. My parents' ancestors were Spanish Jews who fled the Inquisition in Spain and then settled in various places throughout Europe.

My father, Aron, was born in Istanbul, Turkey; my mother, Rebecca, in Castoria, Greece. They immigrated to America in their late teens.

Like so many others before them they came here to

start a better life. I am the youngest of six children, two boys and four girls.

One summer my parents went on a vacation leaving my youngest sister, Zaneta, to care for me. It was the best two weeks of our entire lives together. Zaneta always wanted to be an actress. I saw her act for the first time at Brooklyn College in the play, *The Skin of Our Teeth*. I realize now that her passion for the stage motivated me to become an actor. I remember that around the age of eleven, I began stuttering. It was especially bad when I got excited. Zaneta gave me a book of plays by William Shakespeare and told me to read aloud slowly. She said it might help stop my stutter. It did.

Our family grew up in an Italian-Jewish neighborhood where the kids were tough and street-smart. Some of the kids on my block had nicknames like Billy "Bite-His-Nose-Off" Romano and Johnny "Stuff-Him-in-the-Trunk" Ronzino.

There was one Italian guy who lived in the neighborhood who was so big he wore a crucifix on his neck with a real guy on it. Growing up in a neighborhood like that can be pretty intimidating. But I escaped personal injury because most of the really tough kids thought I was Italian. So they left me alone.

By the time I was born, my father was almost fifty. My mom was in her late forties. Back then, I was called a "change of life" baby, and somehow I had a feeling I'd changed their lives too much. I think my father wasn't too eager to have another kid around at his age. At least that's one of the reasons I've come up with to explain his abusive way of dealing with me. He yelled a lot. Hardly ever spoke in a normal tone of voice.

But my mother and I were very close. I got my sense of humor from her and my love for entertaining people. She loved to cook and to laugh. She had a beautiful voice and she loved to sing. People always asked her to sing at social gatherings and I was so proud of her. She always put herself between me and my father, protecting me as much as she could from his anger. My mother was always there when I needed her and I loved her very much.

Things were different with my father. He was a hard-driving, hard-smoking man who made his living in the garment district of New York. He pressed the clothes, fixed sewing machines, and cut fabric. I loved him, but I feared him. He ruled our house absolutely, and if you didn't obey, you were in big trouble.

His big, loud voice was terrifying when he got mad. He had a bad temper that was hard for him to control. It was on one of those days I felt the brunt of his anger. I was about seven years old.

───────

It was a hot summer day and all the kids on the block had been playing in the water that was gushing out from the fire hydrant. I came into the house naked and wet, with water dripping everywhere. I was just a kid and I felt free and happy being soaked like that.

I started doing a musical riff I'd heard on the radio, performing the two voices and acting out the parts.

"Little boy, why are you going through that revolving door?"

"I'm looking for my Daddy."

"Who's your Daddy?"

"Luke McLuke."

"*I'm* Luke McLuke!"

"Daddy!"

"Son!"

Mom laughed that contagious laugh of hers, but my father screamed at me in Turkish. "Pesavank!"— "son of a bitch!"

He hit me across my behind with a force that broke the skin. The blow was so hard it actually left the imprint of his hand on me. Later, it scabbed up and took weeks to heal. My mother hated him for that... and I wasn't too thrilled with him either.

───────

As I grew older, I tried to understand why my father

was the way he was. He came from a macho culture where the men ruled with an iron fist and the women and children obeyed, or else! He didn't have the sense of humor my mother had. He didn't know how to relax, let his hair down, and have a good time, at least, not around us. He worked hard all his life and spent most of his free time at a coffeehouse up the street, smoking cigarettes, drinking Turkish coffee, and playing cards with his friends.

During the early years of my childhood, my parents regularly observed the Sabbath and my mother kept a kosher house. I attended Hebrew school from ages eight to thirteen, but had a difficult time concentrating on anything other than sports. Rabbi Behar, my teacher, was always quick with the ruler, smacking me across the hands. Corporal punishment was the norm and it wasn't a fun place to be. I attended sporadically, making up all kinds of excuses, telling lies to the Rabbi, who'd tell my father and then I'd catch all kinds of hell. Having a kid around who didn't always follow the rules must have eaten at him in ways I'll never understand.

On Saturday mornings, I would dress up in my Sabbath suit and head over to Russo's Shoe Repair with my Dad to get our shoes shined and then attend prayer service. But other than times such as those, my father and I spent very little time together.

I don't remember him ever taking me to a movie or the beach or any other place a parent usually takes a kid. The only occasion I can remember him ever showing any interest in me was when he took me to the Jewish Community Center on Bay Parkway in Brooklyn to go swimming. That was the only day in my memory that we ever did something together. In those days, there was no such thing as "quality" time.

I made up my mind never to be like him. I wanted my kids to grow up in a house of tolerance and love. I didn't want to have fear in my house. Children should respect their parents, not fear them. I was always afraid of my father's heavy hand, always afraid he'd never love me for what I was.

During the weeks following my accident, that old demon, fear, was back in full force. I was full of terrifying thoughts and feelings, not just of being a quadriplegic, but that no one would want me around anymore. That I would no longer be loved by my wife and my kids. I was afraid my friends would abandon me. That my acting career was over. That I'd end up destitute, unable to provide for my family. That our house would go into foreclosure and we'd be out on the street.

As I lay for hours, days, and weeks in my hospital bed, everything about my past was coming up. I really didn't have much else to do but travel with my memories.

I went through my life, day by day, year by year, trying to understand what had brought me to the day of the accident. I was looking for a reasonable explanation for an accident of fate. I wanted to know why this had happened to me.

But there were no answers, just questions. So I continued to turn my life over and over again in my head, feeling instinctively that if I could grab onto the man I really was, I'd find the inner strength to deal with what had happened to me. I had a long way to go before I could get to the truth of who I was inside, and maybe I never would.

For days, I would relive certain traumas of my childhood. It was as if the pain of the moment made some kind of psychic connection with the pain of the distant past. This kind of inward journey usually led me back to my father. I'd always felt so vulnerable around him, like I'd done something wrong, even when I hadn't. And because I was so totally vulnerable in those early weeks in the hospital, the bad memories were the ones I kept thinking about.

One particularly terrible day, when I was ten years old, my parents and I had just come home from the doctor. My parents had taken me to see a specialist in

New York City because one of my testicles had not dropped. The doctor was giving me injections that were supposed to take care of the problem.

The injections were painful. My arm would get stiff and tender to the touch. When we got home the pain in my arm was excruciating. I was crying and complaining about the pain. For some reason, my father became angry. He grabbed me by the hair and dragged me up the staircase. I screamed and yelled and my mother tried to stop him. He pushed her out of the way.

At times like those, my father would get so angry his lower lip would shake, his face would turn red, and his veins would bulge out. He was like a crazy man. The only thing I could do when he got like that was just take it. Running away would only get me in more trouble. As he continued to drag me up the stairs, he smacked me on the side of the head. My mother pleaded for him to let me go, but he told her to shut up. Next thing I knew, my brother Ben came running up the stairs and got between me and my father.

"What are you doing?" Ben screamed. "Can't you see his arm hurts? Stop hitting him and leave him alone!"

I never saw my father back down before. I think Ben would have hit him if my father hadn't walked away. From that day on, my father was a lot easier on me, and a bond was sealed between my brother and me that made us very close until the day he died.

CHAPTER THREE

THE MAN IN THE GLASS

During the many weeks in the hospital when I was uncertain about my life and my future, there were also some memories that filled me with joy. Most of them centered around my high school days in Brooklyn, when I was very athletic. I think that time stands out so strongly not only because it was one of the happiest times in my life, but because in those days, I was a promising athlete with a lot of physical power. As I lay paralyzed in a hospital bed, it was great to think back on the days when I was young and unstoppable, when strength and flexibility were taken for granted.

I went to Lafayette High School in Bensonhurst, Brooklyn. That's where I met Coach Harry Ostro in 1952, a man who was to have a lasting influence on my life. Coach Ostro was the kind of guy you never forget. I was fourteen years old the first time I saw him, and I remember the day as if it were yesterday. He was an ex-Marine paratrooper with an incredible physique.

He was the toughest-looking man I'd ever seen, with deep, penetrating eyes, a craggy face, and the shortest haircut on earth. He had big, strong, hairy arms like Popeye. The guys on the team called him the Lizard.

He was so intimidating that when he walked down the hallway the students separated, much like Moses parting the Red Sea, allowing Coach Ostro to pass unobstructed. He was all man, and I wanted to be just like him.

To be on his football team was a coveted privilege. His reputation preceded him. He had a string of five years of undefeated football teams. The Frenchies, as they were known, were a mighty force in the Public School Athletic League and it was Coach Ostro's intention that they remain undefeated. He made you work hard. He never let you off the hook for anything, and, if you did make the team, you had to earn the right to stay there.

Football practice was generally held after school. We played on an athletic field that was shared by the baseball and soccer teams. The field was never taken care of, never seeded with grass or watered down to keep the dirt from getting into your nose and throat. Practice lasted three to four hours a day and was a lot like going to war. Many students tried out but only a few stayed with it. It was not easy playing for Coach Ostro. Even the great Sandy Koufax chose to play basketball and baseball instead.

Coach never allowed any player to drink water until practice was over. It sounds crazy, and it was. But it made us stronger, tougher, and meaner, and that carried over to gametime. In the '50s, there were no separate teams for offense and defense. Football players played both offense and defense, a full sixty minutes for each player. We played in equipment that by today's standards was archaic—leather helmets, no face guards. When I look back, I wonder how we did it. But as Coach Ostro loved to say, "No pain, no gain."

He taught a lot by example, and sometimes his way of making an impression could last a lifetime. One day, when I was working out in the football gym, the coach walked in and yelled, "Harpo! Get over here!"

Art's parents, wedding photo. Rebecca (Becky) and Aron (Harry)
Metrano collection

Art's family circa 1925: (L-R) sister Bella, mother, father, sister Lillian, brother Ben
Metrano collection

Arthur "Harpo" Mesistrano,
age 3: Ring bearer for sister
Lillian's wedding
Metrano collection

"Harpo," age 5
Metrano collection

Brown's Hotel, Catskills, 1944. Mom, me, dad (sitting), sisters, Zaneta and Shirley
Metrano collection

Art's mom, Becky, at the Brickman
Hotel singing "Besame Mucho,"
Catskill Mtns., NY, 1947
Metrano collection

Mom and me attending
a wedding, 1957
Metrano collection

Coach and me; I'm on the left, 1954. *Metrano collection*

My first football photo, 1952 *Metrano collection*

Lafayette football squad, 1953.
Team captains Harpo (Art) and
Johnny Ronzino, holding ball
Metrano collection

Art as junior college
all-American, College
of the Pacific
Metrano collection

Lafayette reunion: (L-R) Sid Young, Lenny Mizrahi, Art, Sandy Koufax
Metrano collection

Art performing his "magic" act on the tonight show, 1970. Da-da-da-daaa-da-da-da-da-daaaa.
Metrano collection

THE TONIGHT SHOW
ART METRANO

Card on my dressing room door, NBC-TV, NY, 1970

Carson show, 1971: (L-R) Art, Jane Morgan, Ozzie and Harriet and Johnny *Metrano collection*

Mayor Bradley roast. (L-R) Mayor Bradley, Sammy Davis, Jr., 1975 *Metrano collection*

Becky, Art and Roxanne
(age 3) at our wedding
reception, April 1973
Photo: Andy Chute

Becky's wedding portrait
Photo: Philip Caldwell

Art and Becky
back in the '70s.
High on life?

Art's family, 1987; (clockwise from top) Becky, Art, Roxanne (17), Harry ($2^1/2$), Zoë (9 months) *Photo from Playboy mansion*

Harry (5), Zoë (3)
Photo: Rebecca Metrano

Harry and Zoë, 1991,
playing "dress-up"

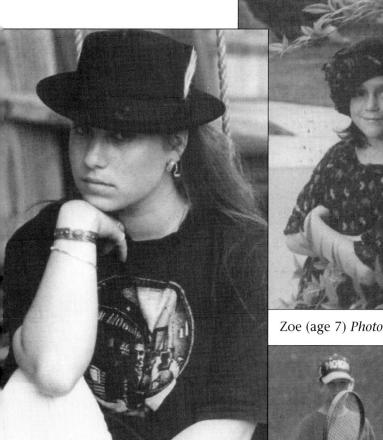

Roxanne (age 21)

Zoe (age 7) *Photo: Roxanne Metrano*

Harry playing tennis, 1993
Metrano collection

My brother Ben and me at Harry's bris (circumcision), 1984 *Photo: Andy Chute*

Art and Becky. Our first dance at Barbara Bingham's wedding, 1990

My Hair, My Hair" – *Police Academy II, 1984 Photo: Warner Brothers*

olice Academy II with Bubba Smith – "Listen, I'm Jewish and you're Black. Can't we et along?" *Photo: Warner Brothers*

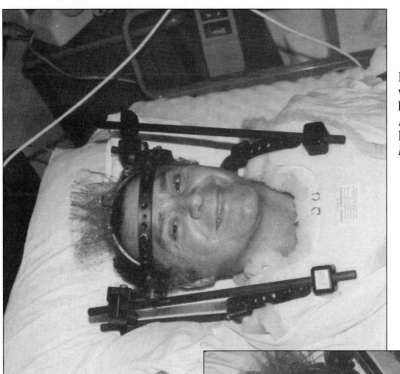

In the hospital,
wearing Zoë's
ballet headdress.
Anything for a
laugh. *Photo:
Rebecca Metrano*

In the hospital after the
fall, 1989, Zoë and me
Photo: Rebecca Metrano

First annual Nite of Comedy, Comedy Store, Hollywood, 1990. (Standing L-R) Jon Voight, Martin Kove-Kneeling, me, Herbie Hancock

Project Support for Spinal Cord Injury
request the pleasure of your company
for a

'Nite Of Comedy'

JEFF ALTMAN, LOUIE ANDERSON, RED BUTTONS, JACK CARTER, NORM CROSBY, RICHARD LEWIS, GENE MITCHENER, CARRIE SNOW, SLICK TRENIER AND OTHER SURPRISE GUESTS.

ART METRANO & FRIENDS

7:30 PM.   SUNDAY, APRIL 21, 1991.   R.S.V.P.

The Comedy Store

8433 SUNSET BOULEVARD, HOLLYWOOD, CALIFORNIA

LIMITED SEATING.   DRAWING FOR DOOR PRIZE THE NIGHT OF THE SHOW.   RETURN BY APRIL 6, 1991.

VALET PARKING.

Invitation to the First Annual Nite of Comedy

Photo from the play, *Twice Blessed*

Reception after Project Support for Spinal Cord Injury Benefit Performance of *Twice Blessed,* with (r) Barry Levinson and (center) Joy Aroff

At Hugh Hefner's birthday party at the Playboy mansion, (L-R) Becky, Art, Mel Torme, Chuck McCann (with plate), Dick Stewart, Hugh Hefner *Photo: John Barr*

Harpo was my nickname in high school. I had blond curly hair as a child and someone thought I looked like Harpo Marx. The name stuck.

Intimidated and eager to please my coach, I stepped forward. Coach Ostro got down on all fours and said,

"Harpo, get on my back!"

I weighed about 215 pounds at the time. Incredulously, I replied,

"Get on your back?"

"Yeah," he said. "Get on my back!"

All the guys in the gym made a circle around us.

Then Coach Ostro proceeded to do twenty perfect push-ups with me on top of him! Completing his task, he stood up with biceps bulging and said, "Now that's how you do push-ups, you phonies!" Then he walked out of the room.

What a piece of work! He challenged our bodies and stimulated our minds. He always made me feel like I could be whatever I wanted to be. He would drill into our heads the necessity of mental and physical discipline. If you played for Coach Ostro, you not only had to be good at the sport, you had to be a good citizen, too.

He was the ideal high school football coach, as interested in building character in his players as he was in a winning season. He made sure before every game that each of us went to our respective church or synagogue to pray for victory. He instilled in all of us the power of God. I wrote a note to God and placed it inside my helmet. It said, "Please God, help me play the game to the best of my ability, and let us come out winners." I left it there for the entire season.

He wanted us to win the game, but he also wanted us to win at life, to get good grades, go to college, and have the careers we wanted. He would remind us constantly of how we should test our limits, and he was always quoting some famous epigram, like:

"Winners are workers and workers are winners," "It's not the size of the dog in the fight, it's the size of the fight in the dog."

With Coach Ostro, these slogans were a way of life.

He knew how to get inside you and teach you that. He was the Vince Lombardi of high school football. He made us feel special by giving us a sense of self-esteem, by teaching us to become achievers without losing ourselves in victory.

He had a poem taped on the wall that he wanted us to live our lives by. It's called "The Man in the Glass."

"When you get what you want in your struggle
    through life,
And the world makes you king for a day,
Just go to the mirror and look at yourself
And see what that man has to say.
It's not your father, your mother, your husband
    or wife,
Who judgment on you must pass.
The fellow whose verdict that counts the most
Is the one staring back from the glass.
You may fool all the world, all down through
    the years,
And get pats on the back as you pass.
But your final reward will be heartaches and
    tears,
If you've cheated the Man in the Glass."
I have always tried to live my life by that poem.

CHAPTER FOUR

POKE ME, PROD ME, BUT TELL ME I'LL WALK

While I waited for a doctor to come to my bedside and tell me the news I'd already heard him tell my wife—that I might end up a quadriplegic—I wondered how I could cope with that. Already, I was having thoughts about giving up. Living in a wheelchair seemed completely impossible for me; I'd had such an active, vigorous life. If what that doctor had told Becky was true, that I might even have to breathe with the help of a ventilator, I wanted my life to be over.

I wondered how I could engineer a way out of this living hell. I couldn't move a muscle in my body, consciousness came and went with the infusion of morphine, and I was in no state of mind to make any rational determination of my future. Yet, the fear of being a cripple, of being a helpless blob in a wheelchair, was so overwhelming that I was already trying to figure out how I could kill myself. A plan for a final exit came to me a few weeks later. At the time, I had no way of doing anything. All I could do was stare at the ceiling and pray.

Patience has never been one of my virtues. I've

always considered myself a man of action, a doer, and waiting around for the doctors to tell me the awful news was not my idea of fun. They pinched and prodded me, X-rayed me, turned me over and under, exam, exam, exam.

But for weeks, they wouldn't tell me anything. The fact is, they didn't know. Spinal cord injuries have a certain mystery attached to them, and even though they had an idea of where my neck and spine were injured, they weren't yet sure of the extent of the damage.

I looked up through the bars of the weird fixture attached to my head. I was wearing a medical apparatus that doctors call a "halo." This large, Frankenstein-like cage encircled my head and was attached to my chest by a plastic vest. It was designed to stabilize the break in my neck, hold fractures together, keep the neck aligned, and promote new growth. I always thought that a halo was something that angels wore. There was nothing angelic about this. It was made of graphite with titanium screws, the same material they make the Stealth Bomber out of. Great, I thought, this way I can go unnoticed in the hospital! Ha!

Later, my neurosurgeon ordered an MRI, a Magnetic Resonance Imaging test. MRI is a technology that images every bone, ligament, organ, and muscle. It has eyes like Superman. It is an extraordinary and frightening procedure.

They slide you inside a coffin-like chamber. The room becomes highly magnetic, and for that reason most metals are not allowed inside. It will turn a Rolex into a Timex.

The next day a transporter named Raul, a young Hispanic, arrived at my bedside.

"Hola, are you Arturo Metrano?" he said to me in heavily accented English. He stared at me for a moment.

"Wait a minute, don't I know you? You look very familiar to me," he said. "You an actor, right?" He paused, "Yeah, I saw you in Police Academy movie. You the guy they always dump on! What happened to you?"

"I fell off a ladder and broke my neck," I replied.

He looked at me and smiled. "That's a tough break. Just kidding," and laughed.

Gloria Estefan blared from his Sony headset as we proceeded down the hallway. I figured he'd go deaf by the time he was twenty-three. As he pushed me down the hall, he was definitely dancing to a different bongo drum. I could only stare at the ceiling lights whizzing by. I felt like I was a time traveler. He knew every nurse in the hospital and gave me a running commentary on their physical attributes.

"You got to see this nurse, man! She got big cucamongas! No! You better not look, you might go blind and you got enough problems!" He laughed again.

We arrived at the MRI where I was delivered to a black technician whom he called Felton.

"Hey, man, I got one for you!"

Felton took one look at my halo and said.

"Raul, what the hell is he doing down here?"

"I got an order to take this guy for an MRI. You recognize him?"

"I don't care who he is... I can't give him an MRI with one of those things on his head."

"I know that... and you know that... but the neurosurgeon... he don't know that." With this comment, Raul lost it completely and laughed hysterically.

"Damn neurosurgeons!" Felton said, "They make eight hundred thousand a year, and they don't know shit. If I give this man an MRI with a halo on, he might arc."

I stared right into Felton's eyes.

"Arc? What does that mean?"

Felton replied, "It's simple, you dumb white man. If you're wearing a halo inside the MRI and it arcs, you fry!"

"Fry?" I asked tentatively.

"Yeah, like southern fried chicken."

Needless to say, I was transported back to my room immediately. As I left, I could hear Felton yell, "You tell the dumb doctor that what you need is a myelogram!"

Raul returned me to my room in the ICU where four nurses placed me carefully back in bed.

————

The word spread fast that I did not get my MRI. This created controversy with the neurosurgeons who insisted that the halo was compatible with the MRI, while Radiology insisted it was not. The resident neurosurgeon, who looked like Dr. Kildare, demanded loudly.

"Take him back down there and get an MRI as ordered!"

I got upset and offered him my solution.

"Take off the halo. Send it through the MRI without me. If it doesn't arc, I'm yours."

Exasperated, young Dr. Kildare stormed out.

Afraid of an insurance problem, the hospital administrator ruled against an MRI. A myelogram was ordered for the next morning. But it wasn't until early evening that another resident arrived to begin the procedure. His job was to inject dye into my spinal cord, so that any damage it may have sustained would be visible in the X-ray that was the second part of the procedure. Thank God Becky was with me. They rolled me over on my right side, using Becky as an assistant. She held onto my butt, while a male nurse held onto my halo and shoulders. Then this tall, thin doctor with an English accent, pulled out a humongous needle, filled it with iodine that they used as the dye, and said, "This will take approximately five minutes."

Bullshit!

Twenty minutes later, he's still stabbing me with the needle! I've got enough holes in my back to start my own golf course.

He finally got the needle in the right spot. Then they rotated the gurney and turned me upside down. I felt like a skydiver without a parachute. Blood was rushing to my head. I had this terrible sensation that I was going to hit the ground head first again. I started screaming like a wild man.

"That's enough! That's enough, damn it! Turn me back up!"

The doctor looked down at me.

"Please, Mister Metrano, I'd appreciate it if you'd just lighten up. We have to wait for the iodine to go from your lumbar region down to the base of your skull, so that when we take the X-ray, we can see the damage to your spinal cord. So please don't scream out, you're frightening the other patients."

"Jolly good, Doctor, but my testicles are in my throat." I couldn't believe his arrogance.

They took the X-ray and wheeled me back to my room. I fell into a dead sleep. About an hour later, I felt someone touching my face. It was Becky. She was crying. Tears were falling from her eyes and landing on my face.

"Honey, the radiologist showed me your X-rays. There are three broken vertebrae in your neck, C1, 2, and 7. But there's no leakage of spinal fluid." Her hands began to shake and her voice trembled.

"Art, that means you won't be a quadriplegic."

I thanked God for the news. As Becky held me, I cried along with her. I knew my life was forever changed by the fall from that ladder.

CHAPTER FIVE

CHAPEL OF LOVE

I proposed to my wife on Christmas Day, 1972. I was thirty-five, she was twenty-four. I told her that if she married me by the end of the year, I could claim her as a deduction. I already had one deduction, my two-year-old daughter, Roxanne. After her mother and I split up, she put Roxanne in a foster home, so I went to court and got sole custody of her.

Three days after my marriage proposal, I picked Becky up from work, drove to the airport, and took a plane to Las Vegas. We hopped in a cab and drove right to the Chapel of Love, a pink building in the center of town. Getting out of the taxi, I turned to the driver and said, "Wait for us; we'll be right out."

Just outside the chapel door, there was a replica of a life-sized bride and groom, the kind that adorns the top of a wedding cake. As we entered the chamber of the justice of the peace, we could hear the Dixie Cups singing, "Gee, I really love you and we're... gon-na get ma-a-ar-ried... Go-in'... to the Cha-pel of Love."

The ceremony began. I said, "I do"; she said, "I do." We were out of there in record time. We jumped back in the cab, back to the airport and back to Los Angeles.

I had met Becky in 1971. She was in the studio where I was rehearsing for a guest appearance on the Jonathan Winters special. She was watching her sisters who were dancers in the show, and I was doing my comedy magic act, "The Amazing Metrano." I liked her the minute I saw her. She had a beautiful face, with a turned-up nose and hazel eyes, and great "cucamongas," as Raul would say.

"What's your name?"

"Becky."

"Becky? That's my mother's name!"

She didn't believe me. She thought it was just a come-on line.

"I swear, it's the truth!" I protested. "What sign are you?"

I've never really been into astrology, but in those days, that's the question everyone asked.

"Gemini," she said.

"Gemini? Really? What day?"

"June 6."

"Becky, you're not going to believe this but June 6 is my mom's birthday... I swear! You've got the same name and the same birthday!"

She laughed, not sure if I was just putting her on, but it was a great line.

"Are you married?" I asked.

"No."

"That's good. Do you fool around?"

"Sometimes."

"That's very good. Where do you live?"

"South Pasadena."

This was not so good. South Pasadena is a long way from Hollywood, where I lived at the time. In the old days, she was what we called GU, Geographically Undesirable. But it really wouldn't have mattered if she'd lived in Alaska. I was hot for her.

I asked her if she'd come to my house for dinner. She said she would. Two weeks later, we had our first date. She drove in from South Pasadena in a beat-up Volkswagen and met me at my house in the Hollywood hills. I love candles and had them lit all over the house. Being a good Catholic girl, when she came in, Becky thought I was holding a Novena... "Hail Mary, full of might, let me sleep with Becky tonight!"

I made my favorite dish, chicken oregano with a side of pasta. We knocked off a bottle of Chardonnay. She laughed at all my jokes. I laughed at hers. Hers were not that funny.

I really felt comfortable with her and she said she felt the same way. By the time we had our fifth date, I knew I wanted to marry her.

We've been together twenty-two years now. We have two beautiful children, Harry, age nine and Zoë, age seven. Becky and I raised my twenty-four-year-old daughter, Roxanne, together.

Like most other couples, we've had our ups and downs. Eight years into our marriage, I began to fool around and got involved with other women. I'm not proud of cheating on my wife, but that's what I did. Naturally, it created tension between us. Becky, who had already exhibited a lack of control where drugs and alcohol were concerned, began her descent into full-blown alcoholism, and pretty soon both of us were completely out of control.

In retrospect, it was a traumatic incident in 1980 which helped to instigate our destructive behavior. I was almost killed, and the stress of that event put tremendous pressure on our marriage. At the time, I was living in the Connaught Towers in New York. I had optioned the rights to "The Little Rascals" and was trying to secure financing to produce it as a Broadway musical. Becky was in Los Angeles with Roxanne, who at that time was only ten years old. Harry and Zoë weren't born yet.

A friend of mine was visiting from Los Angeles and had parked his car overnight in my building's garage. The next morning, he went down to get it, but came back up to the apartment to tell me there was no parking attendant. So I picked up the in-house phone and called Gunther, the doorman. He suggested that we go back downstairs because the building had valet parking and someone should have been there.

When we got down to the garage, the attendant had shown up, and there were a few people waiting in line for their cars. I took Frank's ticket and gave it to the attendant. He asked me for fourteen dollars. I gave him a twenty and he gave me back six dollars change.

He called for the car on the intercom as my friend Frank and I waited. Then the attendant walked back over to us and said he'd made a mistake.

"You was ten minutes over the limit, man. You owe me four more dollars," he said.

I explained to him that Frank had been down for his car earlier, but that no one was around and that I didn't think it was fair for him to charge us the extra amount. He got a funny look in his eyes and said "no problemo." He walked away and headed in the direction of the subterranean garage.

"Hey!" he yelled. "Forget about that guy's car; he don't want it."

Frank got mad and wanted to go after the guy, but I held him back and told him since I lived in the building, I'd handle it.

I walked over to the attendant and told him to call Gunther the doorman and he'd verify everything I'd said. He turned red in the face.

"*I'm* the fuckin' boss down here, not the fuckin' doorman!"

Then he stabbed me in the chest with his pen. I pushed him hard, and he fell backward onto the ground. Meanwhile, blood was oozing all over my shirt.

Another attendant came up from the subterranean garage and saw what had happened.

"Alberto," he said to the attendant who stabbed me, "what's happenin' here?"

"What are you asking *him* for!" I yelled. "This creep just stabbed me!"

Alberto got up and began to taunt me with his fists, like he was going to hit me in the face. Instead, he kicked me in the leg and ran down the ramp to the lower garage. By then, I was really angry, so I ran after him. He tripped and fell. I stood over him, reached into my pocket and threw four dollars in his face.

"Here's your lousy four bucks. Now we'll see who the boss is down here! Hey Frank, call the cops!"

The other attendant tried to make peace by offering to get Frank's car, but it was too late. Alberto was cursing me and I was cursing him.

"I'm gonna get you, you motherfucker!" he yelled.

"Yeah, yeah, screw you, you scumbag." I yelled back.

Alberto walked deeper into the garage while I turned and followed the other attendant to get Frank's car. I'd no sooner turned my back when Frank yelled, "Watch out! He's got a gun!"

I turned around and saw Alberto with a gun in his hand. A shot went off. It sounded like a cannon. The bullet hit the wall. I couldn't believe this guy was gonna kill me over four bucks. I ran for my life! He chased me as I was running out of the garage.

I heard the other attendant yell, "Alberto, don't get crazy!"

I thought it was a little late for that.

He fired the gun again, but missed. I was almost out of the garage when a third shot rang out and he hit me in the leg.

I went down hard, like a buffalo. My leg felt like it was on fire, like there was a man inside it with a blow-torch. I reached down and tugged at my pant leg, pulling it up to look at the wound. My leg began to swell before my eyes, like slow motion photography.

The blood was saturating my leg muscle. I didn't realize it at the time, but the bullet had severed the main artery to my lower leg.

I held my leg in excruciating pain and heard footsteps approach. I looked up and Alberto was standing over me with a maniacal look on his face. He lowered the gun and fired one shot into my right hip and one into my left. I fell forward between my legs and passed out.

I don't know how long I was unconscious, but the

next thing I remember is waking up to hear someone pounding on my head. Alberto was beating me with the butt of the gun! Blood dripped down my face and onto the concrete. I felt like I was gonna vomit! I don't know where I found the strength, but I reached up and grabbed him.

He must've thought I was dead, because the minute I touched him, he started to scream something in Spanish, like I'd scared him. He tried to pull away, but I had a grip on the bastard's shirt and I was stuck to him like Velcro. He pointed the gun at my face and pulled the trigger. Click. No bullet. Alberto ran out of the garage. They took me to Bellevue Hospital and I went into surgery.

The resident doctors on duty, Dr. Manetti and Dr. Seinfeld, comforted me as I slowly inhaled the anesthesia, counting backward from one hundred. I was off in never-never land.

Dr. Seinfeld told me later that while I was under the knife, Dr. Manetti recognized me from numerous appearances on the "Tonight Show." He remembered my comedy magic act. He explained the routine to Dr. Seinfeld. "He's the guy who does the missing leg trick." He then demonstrated the routine while humming my theme song, "Fine and Dandy," "Da-da-da-daaa, Da-da-da-da-daaa." When I awoke, Dr. Seinfeld told me that it was a good thing that they were able to save my leg. Otherwise, I would have been able to do that trick for real.

"Yeah, that would have been really funny." I said.

Ten days later, they caught Alberto. He went to trial, copped a plea and got three years. I almost lost my leg and nearly my life.

Alberto is out of jail now. Last I heard, he was parking cars again in a garage in the Bronx.

For months, I had nightmares about what had happened. I'd wake up in a cold sweat with my heart pounding. That brush with a violent death sent me into a tailspin. I wasn't easy to get along with. I was angry and frustrated and sometimes I took it out on my wife. The fact that Becky was dabbling in recreational drugs and was fast becoming an alcoholic only made things worse. The strain on our marriage was severe. We were both totally out of control.

Our friends didn't suspect how bad things were. We both put up a good front whenever we were out socially. But I was tired of seeing Becky drink the way she did.

I knew our marriage was destined for divorce if we didn't change something soon, but I didn't know what to do. Becky didn't either.

One night after a dinner party with friends, we came home and had a real blowout. "When are you gonna stop doing this to yourself?" I asked.

"Doing what?" she said.

"The drinking!" I yelled.

"I can't help it!" she yelled back.

"You're an alcoholic, you know that? A goddamn alcoholic! If this keeps up our marriage is not gonna last!"

"And what about what you do, Art? You stay out all night, sleep with other women, and you blame me for all your problems! It's not my fault someone shot you!"

We yelled at each other for awhile, unable to get past our own emotional pain. But I was always better at yelling than Becky was. I could always drown her out. I learned how to do that from my father. But then she said something that stopped me cold.

"You want to know what your real problem is Art? You're just like your father."

"What are you talking about?" I said in shock. "I'm not like him. My father hit his wife and kids. I don't do that. I'm *not* like him!"

"Oh yes you are. You're a bully like he was. Everything's gotta be done exactly the way you want it, and if it's not, you lose control and scream and yell like he did. So stop pointing a finger at me and take a good look at yourself!"

I didn't want to accept it at first, but what Becky had said was true. Without even realizing it, I had become a lot like my father, a man I tried to love, but did not want to emulate. I had become a dictator like he was. I gave orders and expected them to be obeyed as if I were a general and Becky were a recruit. I was treating my wife very much like my father had treated my mother. I saw where I had gone wrong, but I knew if we were to save our marriage, I wasn't the only one who had to change.

Becky and I sat in silence for a long time. Then finally, I spoke.

"You're right, Becky. I am a lot like my father. I hate that about myself. I hate it when I scream and yell and act like I know it all. I'm sorry for the way I've treated you at times... I love you, Becky... What are we gonna do?"

We held each other like two frightened children. And then we made a commitment to each other. Becky went to Alcoholics Anonymous and has been sober for eleven years. I sought counseling to help me cope with issues of my own behavior which had contributed to the crisis in our relationship.

Marriage is a challenge for most people. The day-to-day stress of raising kids and making ends meet is never easy. As people get older, their needs often change or boredom sets in and the relationship becomes static and cold. If they can't work out the differences, families break apart. And when a crisis strikes, it tests the limits of love. Fortunately, for Becky and me, we've weathered two major crises and a number of smaller ones. If there's any one thing in my life that's been lucky, it was the day I met my wife.

CHAPTER SIX

HOSPITAL NIGHTMARES

Except for the memory of disorientation and pain, much of those first few days in the hospital was a blur. The CAT scan, the myelogram, and the mishap with the MRI were all preliminaries to a long, arduous process of rehabilitation. I still didn't know the extent of damage to my spinal cord or what the prospects for recovery would be. I was hoping for the best and frightened of the worst.

The toughest part was getting through each day with enough hope to get me into the next. I knew that the likelihood of my being a quadriplegic had been removed when results of the myelogram came back. But paraplegia was still a distinct possibility. Only time would tell how lucky I was really going to be.

After five days in the intensive care unit, I was moved to the acute section of the hospital. Only it's not that cute. Now the rigors of everyday life in the hospital were about to begin.

Late in the afternoon on my first day in the acute section, a nurse came in, checked my vital signs, my intravenous bags, and connected a new IV of glucose and morphine. She then adjusted the tube in my throat and placed a call button in my left hand.

"Ring it if you need assistance," she said. I tried to press it, but couldn't.

"Don't worry," she said cheerily. "Just call out. Someone will hear you. I'll leave the door open."

It sounded reasonable until I realized there was no way I could call out with a tube down my throat. But the morphine began to work its magic and I was soon in a dreamy euphoria.

"Boy," I thought, "that morphine is a real nice drug."

The musical jingle from the old Campbell soup TV commercial popped into my head.

"Mmmmm mmmm good, mmmmm mmmm good, that's what morphine drip is, mmmmmm mmmmm good... "

I even wondered if they could make mentholated morphine... You get high, but you stay cool.

For awhile, I just floated wherever my thoughts took me. I soon fell asleep. I woke up hours later and the room was pitch black. The "high" of the morphine was gone and the darkness of the room scared me.

There wasn't a sound outside my door. Everything was stone still. Then I realized that the door was shut.

"Oh, my God... Why'd they shut me in like this?"

My anxiety level was high. My heart was pounding like crazy. My throat began to swell up and I started to panic. I tried to call out.

"Hello... Is anyone out there... Nurse? Nurse?"

I was barely making a sound. This frightened me even more.

"I need someone... Will you please come in here? I'm afraid to be alone." Still no reply.

"Jesus," I thought. "How could they shut the damn door on me!"

I forced some air out of my throat and tried again.

"Please! Someone help me. I'm in a tomb in here! Buried alive in my own body! I can't press the call button! I can't breathe and can't move! Doesn't anyone hear me? Open the door... Open it!"

Suddenly, light fell into the room as a nurse stepped through the door. The minute I saw her, I flew into a rage.

"Why the hell did you shut the door!"

She tried to comfort me and told me they'd closed it because the janitor was waxing the floor.

"I don't care if someone's waxing the floor! Don't ever do that again! You're supposed to help me—not scare the shit out of me. Fucking hospitals."

She told me not to panic, that it would only make things worse.

"Don't tell me not to panic! You promised you wouldn't shut the door. You lied to me! You lied to me!"

I was out of control. The combination of the morphine and the fear of being in that room alone in the dark drove me over the edge. I was angry that the hospital staff would shut me in like that when I was so helpless. What if I'd had a cardiac arrest? What if I'd choked on the damn tube in my throat? Who would've known?

I felt completely abandoned and I hated having to depend on strangers or anyone else for help. A few minutes later, Becky came into the room. I must have seemed like a frightened child to her.

"Becky, thank God you're here! They shut the door on me! I couldn't ring for help! There was nobody here for me! I was afraid!"

She held my hand and told me everything would be all right.

"Please, Becky... " I pleaded. "I can't be alone like that again. Not until I can press the damn call button. I want my own private nurse here all the time. And I want off the damn morphine!"

The nurse looked at me in surprise.

"The morphine is for the pain." She said.

"I don't care! I wanna *feel* the pain! I wanna feel something! This is my life we're talking about! Please, Becky, help me... "

Becky arranged for me to have a night nurse, and

fortunately, I also got off the morphine. This was an important first step in taking some measure of control over my own destiny.

Some of the most demoralizing experiences for a patient are the feelings of helplessness, of not having a say in what's done to you, or when, or by whom, of being just a body in a bed—a nonperson to whomever walks into the room.

The moment you can express your wishes and have them respected is the moment you can begin to heal, psychologically as well as physically. Healing is only part of the process; the mind has to direct the healing process and cooperate with the expertise of the doctors. A patient's will is a critical element in the healing response. And when a patient feels powerless, his inner resolve to be healed can be obstructed.

I learned through my own ordeal that what goes on inside you is just as important as the medical assistance to your body. I wanted to be involved in what was going to happen to me in the hospital, and I think it's part of the reason I survived. I instinctively knew that if I didn't take responsibility for my own recovery, no one else was going to! While I needed the help of others, I also had to help myself.

It wasn't easy. There are dozens, if not hundreds, of obstacles to self-reliance in a hospital, particularly when you can't move. I couldn't even have a bowel movement without assistance. I couldn't wash myself, feed myself, or do any of the basic things we all take for granted.

In all truth, I was helpless; but I couldn't dwell on that or I'd have never had a reason to wake up in the morning.

Becky was my source of strength. I counted on her for everything. She lived in two places at once—with me in the hospital and at home with the kids. I don't know how she was able to balance their needs with mine, or how she got her own needs met. All I know is, I couldn't have pulled through this without her.

Nothing prepares you for the loss of your mobility.

Most of us think of our ability to move around and walk quickly across the street as a fundamental human right. But for a lot of us, it doesn't work that way.

The way I see it, Life comes along, slaps you in the face, and says, "Let's see what you're really made of, tough guy." There are many people who have it far worse than I, blind people who'll never see, quadriplegics who will never walk. But what happened to them, as tragic as it is, doesn't make it easier for me to deal with the consequences of my injury.

You never really believe it's ever gonna happen to you. It's your next door neighbor, or a stranger you read about in the paper; it's the guy on the eleven o'clock news. It's Magic Johnson, but it's never you.

What, me? Get cancer? Me, have a mastectomy? A brain tumor? Multiple sclerosis? My kid die of AIDS? It's never you. It's always somebody else.

Lying there in the hospital, I kept asking... "Why, why, why?"

Then I thought about this mountain climber who was climbing this gigantic mountain, and suddenly he slipped and began to fall. He was falling so fast, he couldn't believe it. And, as luck would have it, there was a branch sticking out and he grabbed hold of it.

He held on for dear life and yelled, "Somebody please help me! Help me!"

Then from above, he heard a thunderous voice.

"I will help you. Do you have faith?"

"Yes, yes, God, I have faith... I have faith!"

"Then let go of the branch."

In disbelief, the mountain climber replied, "Is there anyone else out there?"

Maybe one of the reasons we don't have the capacity to see the future is that it would make the test of character impossible. One of the many things my accident taught me is that the journey into the unknown takes more than guts. Ultimately, you have to rely on yourself, and that's how you find out what you're really made of.

CHAPTER 7

CRASHING ELEVATORS, SUICIDAL THOUGHTS AND PENILE IMPLANTS

I had been in the acute section of the hospital for all of three hours, when a lady in a white lab coat walked in. She reminded me of Marlena Dietrich. She had an air of mystery about her, and I could tell right away she was an all-business, no-nonsense kind of woman who had come to appraise my situation. I was being put under the microscope again.

"Hello," she said in a sultry European accent. "I'm Dr. Olga Stehlik. I'm your physiatrist."

I immediately got uncomfortable.

"You're in the wrong room," I responded. "I may be paralyzed, but I'm not crazy. I don't need a shrink."

A smile spread across her face and her voice got a bit softer.

"No, no, I'm not a psychiatrist, I'm a *physiatrist*. A doctor of physical medicine."

"What's that?" I asked.

Her face got serious again.

"My job is to manage the treatment and rehabilitation programs of patients with neurological injuries, spinal cord trauma, multiple fractures, amputees."

"Gee, what a pleasant job you have, Doc."

She didn't crack a smile. I could tell she was through with the preliminaries and now it was time to get down to business.

She took out a stainless steel instrument from her pocket. It had a tiny roller on it, serrated like the kitchen instrument used to cut pie crust.

"One side is sharp and the other, dull," she explained. She asked me to close my eyes. "I'm going to touch you with this instrument along different areas of your body. You tell me if it is sharp or dull."

She began sticking me with it.

"Sharp or dull?" she asked.

"I don't know," I replied.

"Sharp or dull?"

"I don't know."

"Sharp or dull?"... "Sharp or dull?"... "Sharp or dull?"

"I don't know, I can't feel it!"

She put the instrument away.

"Can you wiggle your toes for me?"

"I don't think so."

"Try, please." She observed me for a moment and then said, "How about your right hand? Can you move your fingers?"

I tried but I couldn't.

"Try the left."

She gave me a comforting smile. I wondered what she was thinking about, what was going on in her mind. She looked at my chart and said, "I'll be back soon."

———————

My focus shifted as my nose began to itch and I could not scratch it. I began to play a head game with myself. Would I allow the itch to drive me crazy, or would I be able to overcome the sensation mentally? I don't know how long I played the itchy game that day, but during the next two months, I played it over and over again.

During the day, flowers began to fill my room, and every so often a nurse would come in and read the cards and letters. My friends and family had not forgotten me. As I lay there frozen from the neck down, I contemplated my life. The more I contemplated, the deeper my depression became. I was stuck in an 8 x 10 room, while everyone around me was having a life.

Terrible thoughts crept into my brain. I couldn't stop thinking about death. I was losing control of my mind. Different ideas on how I could kill myself began to develop in my head. I prayed to God to take them away, but no matter how hard I tried, I couldn't stop them.

That afternoon, friends came by. Jed and Toby, Larry and Dan, Rabbi Cutler, and Rabbi Gan. Each one tried their best to cheer me up.

They held my hands and rubbed my feet, but I could see in their eyes how upset they were when they looked at me. They all returned many times during my stay in the hospital. Other close friends and some relatives never came and never called. I'll never understand why, but such is life.

Two days later, Dr. Stehlik came through the door once again. Tagging behind her was a young resident who was carrying a clipboard. She had a stethoscope draped around her neck and looked quite officious. As Dr. Stehlik spoke, the young resident wrote down every word.

"I have good news. Your insurance will pay up to 120 days as an inpatient."

What the hell was she talking about? Who asked her anyway? One hundred and twenty days? I'm not going to be in here 120 days. I want to know if I'll ever walk again, and she's figuring out how long I can afford to stay here?

"Listen Dr. Stehlik," I replied, "I'm not going to be here that long."

"I understand, Mr. Metrano. But it's always good to be on the safe side. This is a very costly injury, and I just wanted you to have this information."

I thanked her. She slowly turned around and walked

to the side of the bed and handed the automatic control for the bed to the young resident.

"I'm going to raise the bed and sit you up," she announced. "This will help restore your equilibrium."

Oh, I thought, this should be fun. I'd been flat on my back since the day of the accident.

By now, I'd gotten accustomed to staring at the ceiling, counting the number of cracks and trying to outwit that irritating itch, so the idea of sitting up was attractive. I didn't realize what an ordeal it was going to be.

The protégée pushed the control button and the bed slowly began to rise. I immediately felt weird all over. The sensation of an upward motion was beginning to make me dizzy.

"Slower," I said. "It's got to be slower."

But neither Dr. Stehlik nor her young assistant was listening.

"It's okay, you'll be all right. Just fight it," she said flatly.

But the higher the bed rose, the more dizzy I became. I felt all of my blood leaving my head.

"No, no. You've got to stop!" I said.

"You must fight the dizziness."

"I don't want to fight anything! Put me down!" I was white as a ghost.

"Just breathe, everything will be all right."

"I am breathing, and everything is not all right!"

By then, I was about halfway up. She took hold of my halo with her left hand, put her other hand behind my back, pulled me up, and then pushed my legs over the side of the bed.

The dizziness was overwhelming. I felt like I was in a speeding elevator with the doors wide open and the floors flying by. I thought I would crash through the top of the Cedars-Sinai Medical Center, fly out, and die.

"Please, stop! Put me back down! I'm going to pass out!"

Dr. Stehlik remained in total control.

"Don't panic, don't panic. Just breathe. Breathe! This feeling will pass!"

"It's not passing! Please put me down now!" I screamed.

Firmly, she commanded once again.

"Breathe, you hear me? Breathe!"

Having no alternative, I began to take long, deep breaths. She continued to chant her command, and slowly I began to feel better. She was right. The sensation of vertigo did pass. The imaginary speeding elevator finally stopped. At long last, I was sitting straight up, like Homo Sapiens is supposed to... and I was breathing!

"Gee, Doc, that was a fun ride." I said, imitating her accent. "Maybe ve can go on the Matterhorn together. Then ve can march into Poland, England, France... "

She smiled briefly while the resident made a few notes. I was afraid to ask the inevitable question, but I did anyway.

"So tell me, Doc. Am I gonna walk again?"

I couldn't get an answer from her. Speaking in generalities, she just wouldn't tell me. She wasn't discouraging, but she would say nothing to give me a sense of what my future was to be. The fact is, she didn't know if I would walk again. No one did.

I decided I would figure out a way to save the sleeping pills they had prescribed for me. I'd hoard them away and have a way out in case I needed it. At one time, I had seventy-five of those sleeping beauties. But since I couldn't move my hands yet, I hadn't figured out how to put them in my mouth.

Toying with the idea of suicide gave me a sense of power. I liked having a scheme of deliverance at my disposal. It's a sad irony that one can feel a sense of power by conjuring images of suicide, but by taking that kind of decisive action, I was regaining a sense of control.

Never before had the word "suicide" been a part of my personal vocabulary. I figured people who did that to themselves were cowards. I don't believe that anymore. I can see how desperation and pain drive people to it. And for some, the choice between death and perpetual agony is clear. I will never sit in judgment of those who find their lives so intolerable they end them. Even though everything in me rails against the taking of one's own life, I know that when pain, fear, or hopelessness dominate the emotions, there is often a desire for death.

———————

Soon after, Becky showed up with a suitcase in one hand and a bag of groceries from the health food store in the other. She was Pasadena positive with a perky smile. She was oh so cheerful.

"Hi, honey, how are you feeling?" she asked.

I didn't know how to answer that. I certainly couldn't tell her I'd been contemplating suicide just seconds before she walked into the room. I didn't want to tell her how scared I was either. So I smiled.

"I'm fine, honey. Fine and dandy." Then I hummed the tune of my old magic routine. "Da da da daaaaa..." But I wasn't very convincing.

Becky put a straw in a container of carrot juice.

"Drink this. It'll make you feel better."

Then she held a mirror to my face.

"Art, take a look. I think it's time for a shave."

It was the first time I'd seen myself in the mirror since my accident. Instead of seeing the halo from the inside out, now I was able to see this strange-looking contraption the way everyone else saw it. What a shock. I looked like an old man trapped in a cage.

The screws from the halo were imbedded in my skull and dried blood had caked up around them. My beard was white. My hair had turned gray, and I had a bald spot on top of my head from the fall. I was startled at how much I had aged in such a short time. I didn't recognize the old man staring back at me.

I felt like the poor hero in the movie, *The Man in the Iron Mask*. He was trapped in an iron mask and his beard grew so long, it began to strangle him. I really felt like my life was as surreal as that movie.

My friend Harvey showed up carrying packages of food. Harvey is a guitar-playing, ex-hairdresser, golf-playing actor-model with a sweet soul. He came to entertain me and feed me some macrobiotic soup he had prepared.

"Harvey," I said, "Do you think you could give me a shave?"

"I don't know, Art," he replied. "I've never shaved anyone before."

"Then start with my legs!"

Harvey laughed. Becky took out a razor and shaving cream from the suitcase and handed them to him. Harvey delicately draped a towel around my neck. Reaching carefully between the bars of the halo, he began to shave me. It took him forty-five minutes to do the job. When he was finished, Becky held the mirror back up to my face. I looked a helluva lot better, but my mood wasn't much improved.

As I stared at myself, I thought of "The Man in the Glass," the guy you can never cheat or fool. The more I looked into the mirror, the more I wondered who I was. I had never been a quitter, but this time I was thinking about quitting for good. I was not willing to spend my life in a wheelchair.

Harvey strummed his guitar as my wife put away the mirror and began to unpack the suitcase. She told me about all the various things that were going on at home with our two children. Becky put a picture of Harry and Zoë on the night stand.

"They want to come and see you," she said.

I missed them terribly, but I had not allowed her to bring them to the hospital. I was afraid of how they might react. My oldest daughter, Roxanne, nineteen, had come to visit, and she had handled it pretty well. She was supportive and loving. But Harry was only five and Zoë just three, and I was a frightening sight. At some point, they would have to understand what had happened to me, but I wasn't ready to confront my little children while I looked like some monster.

The next day, the nurses sat me up and strapped me into a cardiac wheelchair so I wouldn't fall out. I began to have prickly sensations all over my body, like my foot had fallen asleep from the neck down. But I was able to move my left thumb slightly.

I suddenly had a surge of hope, but I didn't want to get too excited because I was still completely immobile.

Right after breakfast, a nurse walked in with a big smile on her face.

"Congratulations!" she said.

She walked over and removed the IV from my arm. Then she gently removed the tube in my throat. I didn't feel anything, so I thought, no big deal.

Then she reached for the tube in my penis.

"This might hurt a little," she said.

"Then don't touch it! I'm not kidding!" I said jokingly.

She started pulling the tube out slowly, but I had no sensation at all.

Great, I thought. I can move the thumb in my left hand, but I can't feel anything between my legs. I have a good thumb, but a Dead Dick! And I used to be the jerk-off king of Bensonhurst.

On her way out, the nurse gave me a book called *The Sensuous Wheeler*. She placed it on the night stand next to the picture of Harry and Zoë. It's a how-to sex manual for people with spinal cord injuries. It had diagrams and descriptions for various sexual positions. Some I'd never even thought of, and I thought I'd thought of everything.

With the help of an RN who came to check my vitals, I was given a tour through the book's most provocative pages. My mind went crazy with a thousand sex jokes.

There was a picture of a man with a penile implant. This is a plastic tube they insert into the penis which gives you a permanent erection. A twenty-four-hour hard-on. Boy, I thought, I want one of those! It indicated that when not in use, it fit into a holster that strapped to your leg.

As the nurse turned the page, I thought, maybe it came with a little cowboy outfit. You know, "Have Gun, Will Travel." I sang "Rawhide."

The image of a penis in a holster kept me in hysterics for fifteen minutes. I thought, yeah, and at Halloween, I can go trick-or-treating. "All right, lady, dick 'em up!"

But when the laughter was over, the stark reality of the message in that book sank in. What was the nurse trying to tell me? I figured it was a gentle way of easing me into something no man ever wants to think about. Now I was not only grappling with whether or not I'd be able to walk again, I was having to deal with my sexuality in a way I'd never dreamed of.

As time went by, I thought a lot about human sexuality and why so much of who we are is tied up with what's between our legs. For many people, their entire identity and self-worth are based upon how good they are in bed.

In pop music, on television, and in films, sex is often represented in lustful extravagance or in violent degradation. Rarely do you see a person dealing with impotence, sexual inadequacy, or the challenge of sexuality to someone in a wheelchair.

For me, like most men, sex was an expression of my manhood, as well as my love for my wife. The idea that I'd never be able to function the way I used to was truly frightening.

The world I had entered after falling off a ladder was getting more complicated each day. I was thinking about things that were never part of my experience before. In fact, there was so much to think about, I often felt like my mind was hurtling through outer space, like the starship *Enterprise*, going where no man had gone before, in search of a universe that would be easier to live in than the one in which I was stuck.

But, of course, there was no such escape. For now, there was only uncertainty.

The day after I'd been given *The Sensuous Wheeler*, Becky came bounding into my room with an unusual amount of energy.

"Surprise!"

Standing in the doorway were Roxanne, Harry, and Zoë. Zoë was wearing her ballet tights with a pink tutu and Harry had on his Ghostbuster outfit. Roxanne was dressed like a lady. God, I thought, what beautiful children I have.

"Daddy, Daddy!" Zoë yelled joyfully.

She started to run toward the bed but stopped abruptly and stared at me. It was the first time she had seen Daddy in his monstrous headgear and she didn't know what to make of it. Becky sat down on the bed and we began to make small talk to assure Zoë that everything was okay. Zoë pulled over a chair and stood on it to take a better look.

"It's okay, Zoë," I said. "Get up on the bed."

Slowly she made her way onto the bed and then onto my stomach. To my relief she wasn't afraid of me or the halo. All she wanted to do was hug me.

"What's that thing on your head?" she asked.

"It's my bird cage, Zoë. I'm Tweety Bird and you're Sylvester the cat. Ooooh, I thought I saw a puddy tat!"

She put her little head through the bars of the halo and kissed me.

"I love you, Daddy."

Harry walked over to my bedside and started to play with the screws in my head.

"Does it hurt, Dad?"

I told him it didn't and that he shouldn't worry. Any thought I'd had about my kids being shocked, repelled, or frightened by what had happened to me immediately vanished. They played with my halo, grabbing at the bars. I felt like a human jungle gym. They filled my room with love.

"When are you coming home, Dad?" Harry asked.

"I wish I knew, Harry. I wish I knew."

Later Roxanne took the kids home, and Becky stayed.

"Aren't you glad I brought them?"

"Yes, you did the right thing. You're the best, Becky." She took a good look at me and smiled.

"You know, with your face shaved and your tubes gone, you almost look like a real person."

"Yeah, thanks." I said. "But I still can't feel anything between my legs."

Becky put her arms around me and gave me a kiss. Then she got up and locked the door. She opened my hospital gown and put her hand between my legs and with a big smile, said, "How are you doing, Mister Winkie?"

I was hoping he would answer, but he didn't.

Becky began to massage me and then she made love to me. It was the strangest sensation I've ever had, like an electrical jolt to my system. I couldn't control any of it. My whole body was shaking. My arms and legs stiffened straight out.

For the first time since my injury, I could actually feel life in my body. Mister Winkie wasn't dead after all! He was just in a coma!

———

My attitude took a turn for the better after that afternoon. I knew, beyond a doubt, that I had the support of my family. I guess in the back of my mind, I was worried they wouldn't be there for me. But I was finally able to overcome those fears. It's tough to get through an ordeal like this without the love of your family. Some people have no choice, but fortunately, my family struggled with me and made me feel very loved.

CHAPTER EIGHT

PRIVATE PARTS AND
INTIMATE MATTERS

The day after I was given a copy of *The Sensuous Wheeler,* I was moved out of the acute section and into the Schuman Building, the rehabilitation wing of the hospital. They put me on the eighth floor, room 839, the last door on the right. My room overlooked the world-famous Hard Rock Cafe. To paraphrase Alan Jay Lerner, "On a clear day, you could smell hamburgers forever... "

I was greeted by my primary nurse, Jeannie Wong, an Asian knockout. She was assigned to me for my entire stay in the hospital. For long-term inpatients, the primary nurse becomes a very important daily presence. Jeannie was highly qualified and great to look at. She was on duty in the morning when the bulk of the work takes place. After she left, the afternoon shift took over, followed by the night shift.

Hospitals, like all other institutions, have their own hierarchy and Cedars-Sinai was no exception to the rule. I was really lucky. The caregivers at Cedars were warm and caring. After all, I could have been downtown at County General and I'd heard plenty of horror stories about that place.

Jeannie was always fresh as a flower with a kind word and a smile. Her gentle way of touching me made me feel cared for in a special way. After a few minutes of getting to know each other, her first order of business was to look for bedsores on my tush. Since I'd been flat on my back for so long, the skin on my backside had a few sore spots. Of course, I couldn't feel them so, it was news to me.

As soon as she found the first bedsore, she creamed it and then showed other nurses what to look for. I had fantasized about having beautiful women lust after my body, but having them search and destroy bedsores on my butt was not exactly what I had in mind.

Once the bedsore expedition was over, Jeannie asked me if I'd like to have a sponge bath. I had not been completely bathed since my arrival in the hospital, and I wondered if I was beginning to stink. But nobody seemed to notice if I did. I told Jeannie to go ahead and wash away. She lathered me in soap and water, then she gently sponged me off and in a few minutes, my arms, legs, and chest were squeaky clean.

Then she smiled and asked, "Would you like me to wash your privates?"

"Sure, Jeannie," I said. "And if you wash them real hard, they'll become lieutenants."

She laughed and told me I was a funny man, which was nice to hear, especially since I was lying completely exposed to anyone who happened to walk in.

Then she said politely, "Are you incontinent?"

"No, Jeannie, I've been all over the world."

Again she laughed. "Art, that's not what I mean. What I'm asking is, do you need a diaper?"

I couldn't believe my ears. She was asking me—a fifty-three-year-old man who weighs two hundred and fifteen pounds—if I needed a diaper!

To Jeannie, it was the most ordinary of questions for a man in my condition, but to me it was like a blast of subzero wind had just blown out of the Arctic. To my mind, the only time a person needs a diaper is if he's a Sumo wrestler or doing a TV commercial for Depends.

What she wanted to do, of course, was keep me from soiling myself and the bed sheets. She also wanted to protect me from the humiliation that would follow when someone would have to clean the mess off me. But a diaper is a diaper, and I might as well have been a three-month-old infant for all the control I had over my eliminative functions.

As Jeannie silently wrapped the diaper-like cloth around me, my mind started moving back through time as it had so often during my hospital stay. Suddenly I was eight years old again and I had just wet my bed. For about three years of my childhood, I had a problem with bed-wetting. It's a rather common ailment for a lot of kids, usually caused by stress and other emotional factors.

Like me, most kids grow out of it, but for awhile my nocturnal emissions caused me a lot of grief.

The incident that gripped my attention was a night when my mother had come into my room to make sure I was warm enough. I had wet my bed, but was too scared to do anything about it. A wet bed, if discovered by my father, would mean I'd get yelled at and probably hit. When my mother saw the mess, she put her arm around me.

"It's okay, feeshu," she said. "Don't cry." Feeshu is an old Sephardic word for son. Then she gently helped me take off my wet clothes.

"It's just a little mistake, feeshu. I'll get you some clean pajamas."

But, that night, my father stormed into my room and caught my mother changing the sheets and putting my soiled pajamas in the hamper. She was trying to hide the evidence.

"What's he doing?" he shouted. "Pissing in his bed again?"

He grabbed me by the arm and jerked me off the bed and shook me.

"What the hell's wrong with you? Aren't you ashamed?"

Of course I was ashamed. No kid really wants to

wet his bed, especially when he knows he'll probably be punished for it. My father's angry, insensitive reaction only doubled my humiliation. My mother tried to get him to stop yelling at me, but she could seldom get him to listen.

"It's about time you learned how to use a toilet! You're not a baby anymore!"

With that, he slapped me in the face and pushed my mother against the wall, threatening her with his hand. He dragged me to the toilet and left me there. A moment later, I heard my father's car speed out of the driveway. I started to cry and prayed he wouldn't come back.

Then my mother held me in her arms and rocked me back and forth, singing softly, "Besame, besame mucho... " When she sang, her voice always soothed me and helped me fall asleep.

I could still hear my mother singing when I was suddenly brought back to the present by the agitated sound of a voice I didn't recognize. Jeannie was nowhere in sight and a tough looking, angular nurse was standing over my bed.

"I understand you haven't had a bowel movement in six days," she boomed.

The voice belonged to the eighth floor's no-nonsense, let's-get-down-to-business head nurse. Nurse June did her job efficiently, and without much of a bedside manner. Later, after I got to know her better, I sarcastically called her Nurse Ratchet, after the character from the film *One Flew Over the Cuckoo's Nest.*

Nurse June took the issue of my bowel movements very seriously. Constipation would not be tolerated on her floor. And she was there to ensure compliance.

Who was I to disagree? My stomach was terribly distended by this point, and I certainly needed something done about it. But I wasn't prepared for what came next.

She mixed a glass of orange juice with two large tablespoons of Metamucil. Then she gave me two elephant-sized laxatives, which I swallowed down carefully, making sure the capsules would not lodge in my throat.

With the deft movement of a magician, she pulled a pair of rubber gloves up over her hands, rolled me over on my side, and quickly inserted a "silver bullet" up you-know-where. I felt like Lieutenant Mauser, the character I played in *Police Academy III*, having his first body cavity search.

I mention this rather offensive ordeal because there is no such thing as privacy in a hospital, not when you can't move. Any pride or vanity you come in with has to be left at the door. It may take some getting used to, but for all practical purposes, your body cavities simply don't belong to you. Nothing does.

Once Nurse June had inserted the silver bullet, she sat me up, slid me across a wooden board, and deposited me onto a portable commode disguised to look like a chair. I was hoping she would drape a large cloth over my head so that I could disappear. No sooner had she left the room than a "candy striper," a volunteer, entered, wheeling in my breakfast. Timing is everything!

She peeled the lids off of various foods, exposing a meal barely fit for human consumption. Where was Wolfgang Puck when you need him. She began to feed me. Ah, I thought, in one orifice and out the other. How efficient! The candy striper cheerfully made small talk, wiped my face clean, and left.

A few minutes later, Nurse Rachet walked back into the room and stared down at me.

"Have you evacuated yet?" she said impassively.

"No, I'm still in the room."

I couldn't get a smile out of her. Nothing, nada. I could see that to her, this was a humorless business and any attempt to lighten the mood would go unnoticed. She reworded her question in staccato fashion.

"Did you have a bowel movement?"

"No," I said. "I don't think so."

She looked into the commode. It was empty and she seemed very upset. I had not done my "dooty."

Like magic, the rubber-gloved hand reappeared. She inserted one of her fingers up you-know-where. With the proficiency of a roto-rooter man, she did a quick manipulation.

"Oooh, oooh, oooh," I said. If I could have picked up a phone, I would have dialed the ACLU and filed a sexual harassment complaint.

Ten minutes later, jubilant Jeannie appeared.

"How are we doing, Art? Any luck yet?"

"I think so."

Jeannie was elated as she looked into the container.

"What a good boy! You did good!"

I almost expected her to pinch my cheek and give me a star. But the next thing I knew, she had washed out the commode and was back at my chair with a warm wash cloth.

As she cheerfully washed off my bottom, I looked at this Asian beauty and thought, I must be the last emperor!

When I had a chance to reflect on how Nurse June handled her job and how she handled me, I realized that perhaps there was an understandable logic in her Nurse-Ratchet, all-business method, although I would have preferred a more friendly manner.

Dealing with my inability to help myself in such a personal way was merely a job she had to do. When viewed from that perspective, Nurse June's aloofness had a rationale that worked.

After she had left my room, I lay quietly in my bed, feeling the sun's rays fall across my face. My mind drifted again to a time after college when I was living in New York. I had my own apartment and was trying to make it as an actor.

I was working odd jobs to make ends meet, driving a cab, waiting tables, selling ladies' shoes, when an old friend of mine, an ex-football player who had become a hairdresser, talked me into becoming a hairstylist as well. So in 1958, I bleached my hair blonde and got my cosmetology license and began working at different salons all over Brooklyn.

Eventually, I ended up working for Larry Matthews, an all-night beauty salon at 47th and Broadway in Manhattan. You can imagine the clientele who walked in at midnight to get their hair done—Ladies of the Evening, out to make a buck. They spent it as fast as they made it. They were unbelievably generous, overtipping and sympathetic, warm and loving. It was a wild time in my life. Easy come, easy go. My gay friends were always doing wonderful things for me, knitting me sweaters while at work, cooking extravagant meals on the hot plate in the leg wax room. I look back at those times with great affection. Mostly, I remember one big, happy party. It was one of the few jobs that I really enjoyed.

It was steady income, and my father was happy that I finally had a "real" job. He had never wanted me to be an actor. He thought it was a waste of time.

"You wanna be an actor?" he'd say contemptuously. "Go ahead, be a bum. An actor—what kind of a job is that for a man?"

But I became an actor anyway. At night, I took classes from renowned acting teacher Stella Adler, and when money ran short, I'd style her wigs as a trade-off for acting lessons. Later, I took classes from two of the theatre's most respected professionals, Harold Clurman and John Cassavetes. Eventually, I ended up in the George Q. Lewis comedy workshop, where I was learning how to become a stand-up comic.

I was living on East 87th Street, and on one occasion, my father came up to check out my "pad." I had done a good job of decorating it, and he seemed pleased that I was paying my own bills. I was twenty-four years old, and for once, he seemed impressed with me. We actually had a warm conversation. It was one of only a handful of times I felt like my father actually cared about me. Why had it taken him so long?

My father died during the winter of 1967. One Sunday, my two nephews Irwin and Aaron arrived, banging on my door. I was surprised to see them.

"What's up," I said.

"Papoo died," Irwin said.

For some reason, I smiled. I mean, how could that be? Were they kidding? No, you don't joke about that stuff.

"Really? He's dead?"

They stood there silently. I got dressed in a hurry, and they drove me to Long Beach, New York. My parents had purchased a co-op on the beach overlooking the boardwalk and they had moved there in 1962.

As we drove through the snow-covered streets, I thought about what I had been doing the night before. I was in upstate New York, the Catskill Mountains, performing my comedy act in a second-rate dive, and rather than return to Manhattan and my apartment, I was planning on going directly to visit my parents. I was in my car driving on the thruway, but the snowstorm was so bad, I couldn't see out my window. So I headed back to my apartment instead. How strange. How much does fate play in all of this?

By the time we arrived at my parents' apartment, my father had already been taken to the funeral parlor. Someone told me he had a heart attack in the kitchen. He collapsed on the floor and died. For the first time in my life, I had feelings for my father. I went into "my" room, the one my mother called mine.

She had always hoped I'd move back in with them after they sold the house in Brooklyn. After all, it was on the beach and featured low rent, good food, clean clothes. She reasoned that because I was working on Long Island at the time, it would be so much easier to get to work. Fat chance, Ma. No way. I lived in Manhattan now, upper East Side, just around the corner from the mayor's house, Gracie Mansion.

One by one my sisters showed up. My brother Ben came from the funeral parlor where he had made all the arrangements. Everyone looked frazzled. My mom was crying and my sisters were holding on to each other.

People came to pay their respects and there was

food everywhere. Every Sephardic specialty you could think of sat on every available surface. Sheets were draped over every mirror. My brother pinned a black ribbon on my shirt and cut a slice into it with a scissors.

I couldn't cry that day. I thought, who's gonna take care of Momma now? Is she gonna be okay? At the funeral, I couldn't look in the casket.

I always wanted my father's approval and I never really got it. By the time I had my first break on the "Tonight Show" he was already gone. I wish I could say I really knew my father, but I didn't. But my memory of him has grown softer over the years. He was an angry and sometimes abusive man, but he was also a hard-working guy, who, toward the end of his life, tried in his own way to reach out. I think that's why he showed up at my apartment when he did.

On Thanksgiving Day, 1968, I left New York and drove cross-country heading for la-la land. I sold most of my furniture, including my custom-made round bed. If beds could talk this one would be a blabber mouth. I had a custom round mirror attached to the ceiling to enhance the experience. There was a sticker attached to the mirror that said "objects may appear larger that they really are." I think I'm gonna miss that mirror the most. It was a decadent time in my life, and there was no better place to be than the "Big Apple."

Leaving New York for Los Angeles was an anxious time for me, but I was always one for adventure. My girlfriend Tina and I packed everything into my white "boat"—a '65 Bonneville with rear skirts.

I asked her to drive the first leg of the trip, so I could take photos of the departure. It was a beautiful thing to see, New York City at sunset. As I crossed over the bridge, I was thinking, "I'll be back... I'll be back." New York will always be home.

As soon as we hit the turnpike, a storm was brewing,

and it chased us all the way across the United States. As we entered Missouri, passing under the arch in St. Louis, the sun broke through the clouds. It was an omen of good times a-comin'.

The radio kept us in touch with reports of the terrible storm in the East. Keeping the gas pedal to the floor, I yelled, "Catch us if you can!" The storm lost the race, getting only as far as Texas. Finally, we were in the West, heading for Hollyweird, land of the Stars and the Cars.

In Hollywood, I found a small house on Stanley Hills Drive in Laurel Canyon. I was cutting hair and selling phones to survive. The phone job was a great way into the Hollywood studios. I bought a decal that said Pacific Bell and stuck it on a briefcase. As I approached my first Hollywood studio, Paramount, I was stopped at the gate.

"Can I help you?" the guard asked.

I raised my attaché case, revealing the sticker that proclaimed Pacific Bell. The guard nodded his head and released the wooden barrier, allowing me to drive onto my very first Hollywood lot.

My plan was to knock on every producer's door, try to sell them my product, an automatic dialing system that, when attached to the phone, would speed dial any number from your Rolodex from A to Z. It was almost like having another secretary without the cost. Anyway that was the plan, sell the product, make some money, meet producers and directors, and then show them my 8x10 glossy and phony resumé, and tell them what I was really after—a movie career.

As I lay in my hospital bed remembering incidents in my life I thought I'd long forgotten, I began to feel less alone. I had spent my first day in rehab getting acquainted with a staff of physical therapists and other caregivers whom I knew were there to help me. And even though I was lying in bed in a diaper, I was able to see the humor in it. Who knows, maybe I *could* do a commercial for Depends.

I had joined the ranks of the disabled, but I was

thinking about my career again. What roles could I play? I was hoping my agent would call and tell me I was up for parts in "Rescue 911," "General Hospital," and "I've fallen and I can't get up!"

I knew that I would no longer be able to do slapstick comedy or the physically challenging roles I had done before, but life is definitely a series of compromises, and I was willing to play any role that would keep my career alive. Even if it meant sitting in a wheelchair or walking with crutches. I love to perform. My ego was alive and kicking, and I knew that it would serve me well as I faced the difficult journey that was ahead of me.

CHAPTER NINE

THE JOURNEY BACK

After a day of adjustment to the new environment on the rehab floor, it was now time for me to actually begin the rehabilitation process. It was to be my first day in what I called Therapy 101. While I still felt very little throughout my body, I was put on a program designed to discover just how much, if any, of my mobility I would be able to recover.

Nurse Wong bounced into my room bright and early with her usual pretty smile. She popped a cassette into a tape deck and out came the theme song to *Rocky*. "...trying hard now, getting strong now, gonna fly now." Then she dressed me up in the gym clothes my wife had brought a few days earlier—my Nike shorts, Nike shirt, Nike socks, Nike headband, and Nike sneakers.

It must've been a funny sight—I was all dressed up like a jock and I couldn't move a muscle. The melodic strains of Bill Conti's music and Carol Connors' lyrics filled my room, while I laid there like a lox.

Becky walked into the room, spotted me in my workout clothes and laughed hysterically. I didn't know whether to laugh or cry.

"Sure you're gonna fly now," she joked, "right into a wheelchair."

Nurse Wong raised the bed as far as it could go, then positioned herself to lift me up and off the bed and into the wheelchair. Then Willy, my transporter, wheeled me out of the room and into the hall. I will never forget the impact of that moment. I couldn't believe my eyes. Dozens of immobile patients lined the hall. It was a wheelchair brigade—a group of desolate souls going nowhere.

The wheelchairs were occupied by men and women of all ages, of every race. Some were missing arms or legs, others were stroke victims or had a debilitating disease. It was a gruesome sight. They all seemed depressed and unresponsive to their environment. Some had their heads bowed, while others stared at the wall with vacant eyes, like zombies. I was terrified by what I saw. If they represented the best I could hope for, I knew I was doomed.

This rehab floor looked like a MASH hospital with patients at all stages of the rehabilitation process. Many of them had already lost the battle because they seemed to have lost the will to fight.

That slow journey down the hallway, passing each vacant face, is frozen in time for me. It was emotionally oppressive—so quiet, I wanted to scream.

The sight of so many helpless people can create a tremendous amount of inner stress that has no outlet—except through depression. Every day, the struggle for survival might end in failure for fellow patients, and that can serve to reinforce the desperation others feel. And when the stress is severe enough, it can even lead to suicide. I understand now why this option has its appeal.

The thing you have to always remember is that the battle for recovery starts inside—in the soul. Many of the people I saw that day in the hall seemed like empty shells, as if the life force which animates the body had already departed. I thought of that hallway as the hallway to hell.

As Willy proceeded to wheel me to the elevator, I began to panic. I broke out in a cold sweat.

"No, stop, Willy," I pleaded. "I don't want any part of this."

Willy looked at me with a curious expression on his face.

"Hey, man," he said lightly, "you gotta go down to physical therapy."

"Then take me down another hallway. I can't take this!"

"Sorry, Mister Metrano, but this here's the only way to get to the elevator."

I tried to stay cool, but the more I saw, the more I felt like I was going down Dante's nine circles of torment and into the devil's underworld. I could hear people moaning in pain, see their urine bags hanging beside their wheelchairs. It was a massive assault on the senses, heightened by my own deepening sense of fear.

As we got closer to the elevator, I saw an elderly woman all crippled-up in her wheelchair. She was drooling all over herself.

"Hey!" I yelled. "Why doesn't somebody clean this poor woman up!"

Then I saw a tall young man staring into oblivion, babbling to himself. His head was shaved and he had a huge scar down the side of his head. Suddenly, a pungent odor swept over me.

"What the hell is that smell! Somebody's medication? Is it the disinfectant they use? Oh God, did I shit on myself?"

And then I lost it completely.

"Hey, I can't be on the right floor! You can't put me here with these people! They all look dead! Jesus, I'm in a Coney Island freak house and I'm part of the show! Get me outa here! GET ME OUTA HERE!"

Willy quickly pushed me into the elevator. As the doors closed, I remember seeing all those sad faces staring back at me.

Sometimes only the fear of death will stir the living,

and in the silence of that elevator ride, something happened inside me. I could feel a new resolve take hold of me. I felt a surge of energy rush through my body and my mind was as clear as it had ever been.

"I'm not gonna end up like them," I said to myself. "I'm not gonna quit! Not me. And the hell with suicide! I'm not saving any of those damn sleeping pills! I'm gonna be here for my wife and kids. I'm gonna do whatever it takes to get off this floor and out of this wheelchair!"

I kept rocking back and forth, repeating this over and over again to myself like a mantra. There has never been a moment in my life when I was more determined. The shock of what I saw on my way to the elevator had been so strong that it galvanized me into a mental discipline that changed my perception of everything.

In just a few harrowing minutes, I had made an unalterable commitment to myself: I was *not* going to be a lifeless form shuttled around in a wheelchair. Someone to be ignored or pitied at best, scorned at worst. I was going to stand up for myself and take back my life.

I gave myself permission to fight the good fight, and nothing was gonna stop me. I finally realized that if we spend our lives avoiding pain, we end up avoiding life.

This was the critical turning point on my journey back—the one defining moment that gave me the will to go through the many months of trial and error that followed. As dark and as hellish as the passage down that hallway was, it turned out to be a true blessing in disguise.

CHAPTER TEN

THERAPY 101

The elevator doors opened and Willy wheeled me into the physical therapy inpatient facility. He handed the woman behind the desk some papers, and as she looked them over, Willy turned my wheelchair and left me facing the wall. He then locked the wheels and disappeared.

I wondered why he just left me there facing a blank wall. There were other places he could have placed the wheelchair. There was a window close by. It would've been nice to be able to see people walking by instead of staring at a blank wall. But since I was incapable of moving the wheelchair myself, all I could do was stare at the greenish paint on the wall and get angry that Willy had left me sitting there like a vegetable.

Next thing I knew, other patients were being wheeled in, parked alongside me, and also left facing the wall. We were like parcels somebody left at the door. I tried to make eye contact with a couple of the other patients, but they all kept their heads down or stared straight ahead. I really didn't like the treatment we were getting.

"Excuse me," I said to the wall. "Will someone

please turn me around?" I couldn't be sure if anyone behind the desk heard me.

"Hello? Is anybody there? Please, I don't like facing the wall."

A friendly black woman walked over, took my chart from the back of my wheelchair, turned me around. Her name was Lulu and she recognized me from years before.

After I'd been shot in New York by the maniacal garage attendant, I had come back to Los Angeles and had been placed in a physical therapy program at Cedars-Sinai. Lulu had been my therapist! It had been so many years ago that, at first, I didn't recognize her until she gave me a big-toothed grin which revealed two gold teeth in the front of her mouth.

"Ah, Lulu!" I said, remembering her golden grin.

"What are you doin' back here? What happened to you?" she said.

I told her about my accident. She shook her head side to side.

"My poor boy, what am I gonna do with you?"

"Get me better, I hope."

"Well, you've come to the right place," she said assuredly.

We spent a few minutes catching up on each other's lives and then she wheeled me over to meet my physical therapist.

Her name was Mary Beth. She was six feet tall, young, strong, a Viking of a woman, and she took absolutely no flack from anyone.

Mary Beth was a dedicated therapist, and with her, you worked hard whether you wanted to or not. She had endless patience. Her mission was to get you ambulatory as fast as possible, and she took her job very seriously.

In rehab jargon, your physical therapist is your PT, but to me PT also stood for physical terrorist, especially when I had had a particularly tough workout. That is what I would call her. Even though Mary Beth was definitely a hard driver and she worked my tail off, I was secretly glad she did. I knew she was as committed as I was to my getting on my feet again.

But at the beginning, I didn't realize just how much of a reign of terror my physical therapy was going to be. In the first few minutes, Mary Beth promptly introduced me to a new concept in physical pain.

She got me out of the wheelchair, put me on a mat and rolled me over on my stomach. I felt like a beached whale. I had trouble breathing and had extreme pain in my arms and shoulders. I was beginning to cramp everywhere. My pelvis hurt. My ass hurt. Everything hurt.

Mary Beth quickly turned me over onto my back and massaged my arms and legs. I started to have spasms, my arms and legs shaking uncontrollably. I felt like a piece of bacon cooking on a grill. All that was missing was the sound of the sizzle.

"Did you take your meds?" she asked.

"Yes-s-s-s," I replied as I lay there doing my dance.

"Tell your brain to quiet your body down," she said. Slowly, the shaking subsided. She began checking me for strength and flexibility.

I had been stationary for only ten days, and already my muscle strength had deteriorated and my shoulders and arms had begun to atrophy. The spinal cord is encased in three layers of membranes; together with the brain, the spinal cord constitutes the central nervous system. The moment it becomes damaged, everything shuts down. The muscles lose tone and wither.

Mary Beth grabbed hold of my legs with a motion that seemed choreographed. Her hands were quick and elegant in the way they moved. She reminded me of those guys in classic Italian pizza parlors. They spin the dough around in a circle, throw it up in the air, catch it, then massage it with precision.

She rolled me over again, and I was on my back. I got dizzy, so she sat me up. I wasn't good at keeping my balance, and every time I leaned over, she would straighten me up. I was constantly leaning to the left, then the right. I called myself the Leaning Tower of Metrano.

She continued to manipulate me, moving my legs back and forth, stretching my fingers wide open, opening my hands. But my hands kept curling up into a fist. Mary Beth kept at it, holding my hands down with both her hands.

"Just relax, Art," she said. "Tell your brain to tell your hands to relax."

"I'll try."

"Take a deep breath. Relax. Concentrate."

She removed her hands from mine. It didn't work. My hands seemed to have a mind of their own.

Mary Beth lifted me off the mat and onto the parallel bars. I was continually amazed at the strength and dexterity of my PTs, who were mostly women. They moved me around like the queen on a chessboard.

Once she got me up, Mary Beth put a velcro belt with large loops around me and held onto it. Lulu assisted her and placed my hands on the bars and opened them so I could get my fingers around them. My body was numb, and I didn't actually feel the bars or the floor against my feet. I was completely propped up by gadgets and by Mary Beth. But, I was out of the wheelchair!

At the far end of the parallel bars was a full-length mirror. Someday, I hoped I'd be able to walk the length of the bars without help. I knew it was a long way off, but now I had something specific to work for.

Right after PT, I was sent to OT—Occupational Therapy, the other facet of the rehabilitation system. Each therapy has its own objectives. A physical therapist works to relieve pain, improve muscle strength and mobility, and to improve basic motor functions, such as standing, walking, and using crutches.

An occupational therapist works to help the disabled recover physical competence. The OTs teach you everything from how to pull up your zipper to how to get in and out of a shower. They create amazing adaptations to make life easier—like a wooden pole with a hook on the end so you can pull up your shorts, or a large ring around your zipper so you can pull up your fly, or sponge cylinders to put around your utensils to make them easier to grasp. That's why the sign over the door of the OT room said, "OCCUPATIONAL THERAPY IS THE BRIDGE TO INDEPENDENCE."

By the end of my first day in PT and OT, I was utterly exhausted, and my therapists had done most of the work! Although I was anxious to work hard and progress, I was also trying to fight off another bout of depression.

The next day I was fitted for a special glove for a swollen right hand, called a compression glove. It blew in air and helped reduce the swelling. I was also fitted for tech hose, which I can best describe as a very serious type of pantyhose that keep you from getting thrombosis due to lack of leg motion.

At night, I had to wear a pair of very strange-looking white plastic boots, lined with fluffy material, which I called my bunny boots. They were designed to keep my feet at a ninety degree angle while I slept. I wore a hand-splint so my fingers wouldn't curl up and stay that way. For months, I was attached to all kinds of gadgets designed to teach my body how to function again.

One day turned into another, and it was the same routine over and over. I woke up at 7 a.m. The nurse took my vitals, fed me breakfast, slid me across a wooden slat from the bed to the commode, gave me a suppository, cleaned me up, dressed me, and then sent me off to physical and occupational therapy. The next day, we'd start all over again.

I spent forty-eight days in the rehab as an inpatient. Day to day progress was slow, but steady, one step at a time. I had daily battles with a knife and a fork.

Before my accident, I was able to bench press 260 pounds. I used to do curls with 50-pound weights in each hand, but now I couldn't even lift a donut, scratch an itch, or wipe my own ass. Every third day, they had to tighten the screws in my halo, and that hurt like hell. Each day the puncture wounds had to be disinfected.

But the long and slow process of rehabilitation developed, and very gradually I began to regain strength and mobility. My body was responding to the therapy, although I couldn't walk without a major amount of support from Mary Beth and Lulu. Just how far therapy would take me was still an unknown.

From my first day in rehab, my goal was to be able to walk again. I kept that vision alive inside me, and whenever I felt myself getting depressed or tired, I'd think of how far I'd come and of how much I wanted to be active again. I'd think of my wife and kids and how much I wanted to do things with them. I didn't want to be a burden to them. I wanted to hold my children in my arms again. That's what kept me going when the pain of therapy or the boredom of hospital life got to me.

CHAPTER ELEVEN

HOSPITAL ADVENTURES AND THE CAMARADERIE OF STRANGERS

I used to look out my hospital window and stare at the sky, and I'd think about Roy Campanella, Teddy Pendergras, Mark Buoniconti, and Darryl Stingley. They each had devastating spinal cord injuries that have altered their lives. Somehow, I felt connected to them, as if I knew them because we'd experienced a similar kind of loss. Before my accident, a person in a wheelchair was outside of my world. We weren't running the same race. But now I'm disabled and I feel their pain.

Inside every person in a wheelchair is a story of daily struggle, not only with their disability, but with the attitudes of strangers. It's often hard to shake off the way some people react to the sight of a wheelchair. It might be a subtle turning away of the eyes or patronizing small-talk about how brave one is.

My way of dealing with that kind of stress, along with the rehabilitation process, was through humor. Once I had made the commitment to do whatever it took to walk again, I decided I'd become the court jester to the wheelchair brigade.

I'd bring out the best in them with my bravado personality in my staccato body. All of us had broken-down bodies that needed fixing, and I decided to find the humor in it.

I started with my halo. My children decorated it with different color rhinestones and a star of David front and center. My nurses hung cotton balls from it, like a Mexican-American low-rider Chevy. It was hysterical. My comrades thought I was the funniest thing on wheels.

So I became known as the "Smile Doctor" of the Rehab Center because I could make people laugh. I thought if I could continue to do that, I'd be helping people heal. A funny thing happened along the way, it helped *me* heal. Making fun of my own paralysis enabled me to stop entertaining the suicidal thoughts I had been having.

The next day, Willy took me down to therapy. I said hello to everyone as we passed by. They were all sitting in the hallway in their wheelchairs watching me. As we made our way down the hall, my oddball sense of humor put smiles on their faces.

When we got close to the elevator, I saw this sweet little old lady sitting all alone. She was black and blue from head to toe, nasty bruises everywhere. The name tag on the back of her wheelchair was hanging sideways.

"Hello, Mrs. Nordlinger, how are you?" I said with a big smile. She looked up and stared at me as if to say, Who's this crazy person talking to me?

I just kept smiling. "What happened to you?"

"I was in a car accident and went through the windshield," she said in a shaky voice.

"Nice color you have," I said, referring to her black and blues.

She grinned at me.

"Don't worry," I said. "You'll be out of here in no time."

As Willy pushed me down the hallway, she nodded and gave me a little wave of her hand. I threw a kiss back to her.

The eighth floor was full of all kinds of interesting characters with whom I am still friends today.

One of the most endearing people I met was Marcus, a tall young man from Switzerland. He was very shy and often walked the halls aimlessly. He had few visitors and was alone most of the time. He'd had an operation for a brain tumor, and as a result, his head had been shaved and there was a very large scar down his right temple to the nape of his neck. He wandered by my room every now and then with a strange look in his eyes, so one day I invited him in.

He seemed worried and uncomfortable. I asked him if he was okay. He told me he was having trouble with his eyesight.

"I can't see," he said. "I can't even see your face." He was sitting less than three feet away from me.

"Well, I look just like Mel Gibson."

He smiled. I asked him why he couldn't see anything and he told me his glasses were broken.

"So, why don't you get new ones?" I said.

"I'd like to, but I can't get anyone to get them for me. I've been like this for three weeks."

I called the nurse and asked her to help him. I just couldn't believe the poor guy wasn't being looked after. In a few days, he had new glasses and that strange look in his eyes disappeared. When he came by to thank me, he seemed ill at ease again.

"I think I'm going deaf," he said. "I think they hurt me during the operation."

This time I asked the nurse to get him an ear specialist. The specialist came into my room, and with a wire probe pulled out of Marcus's ear a brown glob the size of a peanut. It was a cotton ball completely waxed-over!

The next day, they took Marcus down to the ear doctor, who removed a few more cotton balls that were left in his ear during the operation. Finally, Marcus could hear clearly again! In forty-eight hours I had helped a fellow patient to see and hear again. I felt like one of those faith healers on TV. "You can see! You can hear." But I still couldn't walk.

Marcus couldn't stop thanking me. All the guy needed was for someone to pay a little more attention to his needs. Sometimes patients are fearful and ashamed to talk about their problems. They don't know how to speak up for themselves. They accept their infirmity as a *fait accompli*. And for someone as shy as Marcus, that could be dangerous. I was pleased that I was able to help out.

That night I began to let go of my own pain and see the pain of others. I think this is an important part of the healing process—to realize that you're not alone in the struggle and that we're all connected to life by the same emotions. I felt connected to everyone on my rehab floor. We were all fighting the same battle, whether or not we were in wheelchairs. We all wanted to be whole again, in body and spirit. That's a monumental task, even when you're healthy, but when you're seriously ill with a disease or have been injured, it's even tougher.

As I lay in bed thinking, I could hear the patient in the room next door coughing. Rhoda was in her late fifties and she'd had a stroke. She was confined to a wheelchair; her right arm was partially paralyzed and she couldn't unbend it. During the day, I seldom heard her make a sound, but at night, she coughed and coughed.

Rhoda and I shared the bathroom that connected our rooms, a bathroom that neither one of us could use! And between us there was only one commode that we both needed.

Whenever she wasn't around, I would have a volunteer sneak into her room and steal the commode. It was a running joke between us. In the morning, she'd wake up, look around for the commode, and have to yell out.

"Okay, Art, what'd you do with my commode?"

I would shout back.

"It's mine and you can't have it."

It always made her laugh. Some people play musical chairs—we played musical commode.

I had an affinity for Rhoda and I wanted her to be able to use her arm again. I kept yelling at her.

"C'mon, Rhoda! Straighten your arm! How are you gonna pitch in Saturday's game. I'm looking for a strike, not a stroke!" She mumbled something incoherent.

"Hey, Rhoda," I said. "Aren't hospitals great? Where else can you get three meals a day, all the drugs you want, and they expect you to pee in your bed?"

"Yeah, and I'm peeing right now!" she laughed.

As far as I could tell, I swear that's what she said. And she had me laughing, too.

About midway through my stay in rehab, I tried to raise the spirits of an older black man who'd had both his legs amputated. He was a chronic complainer and drove all the PTs crazy.

He was being fitted for prostheses that he said were never going to work. Every day, he went through the same tirade. He was upset with what had happened to him and didn't know how to let go of his anger.

"How're your new legs coming?" I asked. He started to complain again.

"Oh stop bitching. Of course they're gonna work. You don't wanna be the first black man who can't jump, do ya?"

He smiled.

"I'll buy you a pair of Nikes when you get your new legs on."

He didn't say anything, but I knew I'd broken the ice.

A few days later we were exercising on the same mat together. Mister Johnson was still moaning and groaning about his problems, so I started singing.

"Nobody knows the trouble I've seen; nobody knows my sorrow... " He cracked a big grin and he gave me a "low five" because I couldn't raise my arm.

A couple of days later, we passed each other in the hall.

"How're you doin', Mr. Johnson?"

"Let me tell you something, son. I don't have a leg to stand on."

We both laughed, leaned forward in our wheelchairs and embraced. I'd made another new friend.

———

While I was in the hospital, I saw a lot of friends at all hours of the night. On one occasion, my friend Harvey came by after playing his guitar in a cabaret. It was midnight and he wanted to see if I was up and needed company.

"Sure, I'm up. You think I can sleep with this thing attached to my head? What's going on?"

"There's a famous actor who has been admitted to the hospital," Harvey said.

"Who?"

"I'm not sure," he replied. "But he used to be in those swashbuckling movies of the forties."

"Cornel Wilde?" I said.

"Yeah. How'd you guess that?"

"He's a friend of mine. Let's go see him."

Harvey helped me out of bed and into my wheelchair. When we arrived at the nurses' station, the night nurse asked, "And where are we going so late at night?"

"There's a friend of mine in the hospital. Maybe you can tell me where he is. His name is Cornel Wilde," I said.

She looked him up in the directory and gave us a map to his room. He was in the East Tower of the hospital, a fifteen minute ride by wheelchair. After taking two different elevators, we finally arrived at our destination.

There were people gathered in the hallway. I recognized some of them. Skip E. Lowe, a local cable talk show host approached me.

"What happened to you, Art?" Skip E. asked.

"I fell off a ladder and broke my neck."

"Oh, my God," he replied.

"How's Cornel?"

"Not good. He's dying. He has leukemia."

I was sorry to hear it. From 1985 until the time of my accident, I spent many evenings up at Hugh Hefner's mansion talking with Cornel about the old days in Hollywood. We would dine and watch old movies in the screening room, and he would tell me great stories about the actors and actresses he had worked with. All this flashed through my mind as Harvey wheeled me into Cornel's room. People stood quietly against the walls. Seeing me with my halo startled some. They stared at me.

Cornel was lying on his bed, tubes sticking out from everywhere. His breathing was labored and loud. I advised one of his friends who was standing closest to his bedside to raise the head of the bed with the control button.

"I don't think we're supposed to move him," he said.

"Just do it," I said. "He'll breathe better."

As the bed was adjusted, his breathing became quieter.

"How'd you know that?" someone mused.

"You learn these things when you're a patient," I said.

I raised my voice so that Cornel could hear me.

"It's Metrano. How are you doing, Cornel?"

He raised his left hand and gave me a thumbs up! Everyone in the room was amazed. They told me he hadn't responded to anyone for days. I stayed a while longer holding his hand. I am very grateful for the time I spent with Cornel. He died the next day.

During the course of my rehab, I thought a lot about Cornel. He'd been such an active man, and in his films he always displayed amazing physical dexterity. He swung from balconies and did all of his own stunts. I only wished I could do that in real life.

I was in physical therapy for six weeks before I

attempted to walk between the parallel bars without assistance. I could barely put one foot in front of the other and I was holding on for dear life. I felt like a Flamenco dancer on a cruise ship. My brain was sending messages to walk, but my legs weren't receiving. Nonetheless, it was a milestone in my recovery.

From the parallel bars, I graduated to a stationary walker with no wheels, and then to a walker with wheels. The big breakthrough came much later, when I finally graduated from the wheelchair to a pair of Larfshed crutches. And then to one crutch.

Throughout the rehabilitation process, the doctors, nurses, and therapists prepared me for the new journey I was about to undertake. My special friends on the rehab floor were my day-to-day companions, fellow travelers on the long and arduous road to a new life.

CHAPTER TWELVE

IT'S NOT OVER
'TIL IT'S OVER

I was released from the hospital on November 17, 1989, exactly two months from the day of my accident. The halo was still attached to my skull and my rehabilitation process was still far from over. The fact is, I'll be an outpatient as long as I live.

Where the PTs and the OTs had finished, Becky would have to take over. When I first came home, things were difficult for all of us. I still couldn't shave, shower, or handle my bodily functions alone. I couldn't dress myself and I still had to use the wheelchair. We had to install a chair and special fixtures in the shower so I could help myself get in and out without falling. We had to remove the screen door so I could get in and out of the house. There were dozens of adjustments that had to be made.

I tired easily and my presence in the house was a strain on everyone for a while. I was glad to be back with my wife and kids and they were glad to have me back, but things were very different from before. I needed a lot of help getting around, and Becky had to be my assistant. I knew it wasn't easy for her, but she rarely complained.

And when she did, it was only because I was being too demanding. In spite of the chaos, Harry and Zoë understood. Kids know so much more than we give them credit for.

Two weeks after my release from the hospital, on the day after Thanksgiving, the doctors finally removed the halo from my skull. "Free at last, free at last; thank God Almighty, I'm free at last!"

A month later on December 28, Becky and I celebrated our wedding anniversary, and I was planning to take her out for a romantic dinner. But first, I had a follow-up visit with my neurosurgeon. I had gone to a radiologist a few days before for an MRI, the test I wasn't able to have before while I was wearing the halo. The neurosurgeon had received the results of the MRI, and we were going to discuss how well my neck had healed.

Becky and I were sitting in the waiting room when the nurse called us into the examination room. My neurosurgeon came in with the results of the MRI. He had a troubled look on his face.

"Well, Doc, how's my new neck?"

"Art, you've got the worst-looking neck I've ever seen," he said without hesitation. I turned to Becky.

"Hey, honey, a neurosurgeon with a sense of humor."

"There's nothing funny about this, Art," he said.

"Here, look at this." He pointed to my MRI findings.

"You see this? Your spinal cord is half the size it should be. You're going to need surgery."

I stared at him in disbelief.

"Surgery! I've been wearing a damn halo brace for over three months! Now you tell me I need surgery!"

He paused for a moment, then pointed at the MRI again.

"Art, there's a large calcium deposit, what we call a spur, pressing in on your vertebrae—on C2 and C3. If someone were just to pat you on the back, it could sever your spinal column and then you'd be a quadriplegic for sure. I want you back in the hospital immediately."

Becky and I sat there in shocked silence. Everything seems to be going so well and then, bam... it's a crisis again. I turned to her and said morosely, "Happy anniversary, Becky."

The next evening, Becky and I were sitting in bed talking about my upcoming surgery. Our son Harry came into the bedroom and said his neck hurt. We examined him and he seemed fine. But the following day, he was running a fever and his neck was swollen. Becky took him to their pediatrician, who gave him an injection of antibiotics and a prescription for more of the same.

I couldn't help but think it strange that my son was having some kind of neck problem just as I was about to have surgery on mine. I had an eerie feeling, and I didn't like what was happening.

On New Year's Eve, Harry's fever had elevated to 104 degrees and the antibiotics didn't seem to be working. His neck had swollen like the Goodyear blimp. Becky rushed him to the doctor, who then referred us to Dr. Lee, a pediatric ear, nose, and throat specialist at Santa Monica Hospital.

Dr. Lee examined Harry and immediately admitted him into the hospital. He was given antibiotics and glucose intravenously. His pain was worse, he couldn't swallow, and he couldn't turn his head. In three short days, my athletic little boy had become a very sick child, and no one knew why.

Becky stayed with Harry at the hospital. Zoë and I came by every day to cheer him up. A few days later, my wife and I had a conference with Dr. Lee. The swelling in his neck was not responding to antibiotics. He told us Harry needed an MRI, the very same test I'd had just a week earlier.

"An MRI?" I asked. "What for?"

"Because," the doctor said carefully. "We want to rule out lymphoma." He kept talking, but I stopped listening. All I could hear was the word LYMPHOMA. LYMPHOMA? It screamed in my ear. I felt like someone had just hit me in the stomach with a baseball bat. The idea of my son having cancer sent us into a tailspin.

That afternoon, Becky came down with the flu. She was on an emotional roller-coaster ride, first with me and now with our son, Harry. Getting through my problems was a breeze compared to what was happening to our little boy. I sent her home and took over the hospital duties.

I thought I had made my peace with myself and the unfairness of life. I thought I had finally come to terms with my own near-fatal accident and all the pain it had caused for both me and my family. But when Harry got sick, the inner peace I thought I had developed was shattered. I railed against God and life and all that makes human beings suffer.

I lost all sense of perspective and wanted to lash out, only I didn't know at whom or at what. All I knew was that my son was in trouble and anything that I had been through was nothing compared to the thought that my child might die before I did.

I went into Harry's room. He was sleeping. I got down on my knees next to his bed and screamed at God.

"God, stop screwing around! Do whatever you want with me, but please, don't take my son. He's just a little boy."

On New Year's Day, 1990, my neurosurgeon called me and asked me why I hadn't checked into the hospital. I told him my son was in the hospital and that being with him was more important.

"Look, Art, you're taking a helluva chance. Call me when you're ready, and be careful."

To my mind, there was nothing heroic in denying

myself the surgery I needed at that moment. I just wanted to be sure Harry was all right, and I wanted to be there if he needed me.

On January 2, the results of Harry's MRI came in.

It showed a large mass in his lymph area. The doctors had to go in and do a biopsy. I explained the procedure to my son. He looked at me with those big brown eyes.

"It's okay, Dad. I'm not afraid. I know I'll get better, just like you did when you were in the hospital."

I was sure glad one of us was brave.

A day later, they performed surgery and removed a growth behind his left tonsil. They did three tests to determine if the growth was malignant. The first two came back within a couple of hours. Negative. No cancer. But we'd have to wait another day for the third result.

At 3:30 a.m., I was in Harry's room, wide awake and scared to death. Harry tossed and turned in his sleep, and the IV had come out of his arm. I called the nurse and she found a new vein and stuck in the needle. It was the first time Harry cried since he'd been in the hospital.

"It's okay to cry, Harry. Cry as much as you want."

I climbed into bed with my son, held him in my arms, rocked him back and forth, and sang to him, just like my mother did when I was a little boy.

It seemed as though my life had come full circle at that moment, and I had come to a new place. I was just an ordinary father trying to comfort his son, but I realized right then and there how little we appreciate the ordinary in life. My own father never seemed to understand this. Maybe that's why he never held me or told me that he loved me. Harry, Zoë, and I have a bond that my father and I never shared, and for that I'm very grateful.

The following morning, the final biopsy result was in.

Harry's doctor stopped me in the hallway.

"It was a very bad abscess, Mr. Metrano, but your worries are over. There's no malignancy."

We never knew what exactly had caused the swelling in my son's neck or why it was such a puzzle to the doctors. It was simply one of those medical mysteries that often befall a child and there's nothing you can do about it. But I thank God every day that nothing ever came of it.

———————

Once I was sure my son was out of danger, I called my neurosurgeon and Becky packed my bag and drove me to Century City Hospital. They have a unique microsurgery unit designed for the kind of precision surgery necessary for my neck. Doctors opened up the right side of my neck, took a bone from my hip, widened my spinal column, removed the spur, and fused me back together.

It's never over 'til it's over.

CHAPTER THIRTEEN

A LIFE RECLAIMED

I left my wife and kids one morning to work on a house we had up for sale. I fell off a ladder and broke my neck. Doctors call it the Hangman's Break. Today, I dream about playing baseball with Harry. I'd love to carry Zoë on my shoulders. I'd like to walk down the aisle with Roxanne on her wedding day. I'd love to go dancing with Becky, but I can't. And that's okay. I don't ask God for those things anymore, just to show me the way. I'm lucky to be alive and lucky that the fall didn't leave me completely paralyzed.

I fought hard for my comeback. Today, I have about seventy percent of my mobility, and I walk with a crutch. Nothing in my life has been the same since I fell off that ladder. My physical limitations have been offset by a better understanding of how to live my life. I value my family in ways I never did before. I spend more time with my children now, and I better understand the treasures of watching them grow. I know how important it is to respect their individuality, as well as love them.

Becky and I have grown closer. My accident forced us both to go on an inner journey to rediscover ourselves and our marriage. It didn't come easily. We worked hard to overcome the obstacles that got in the way.

The accident caused a family crisis, and because of that crisis, we were forced to examine who we are and what we are to each other. It's been a life-affirming experience that has given me a much better perspective on so many of life's tough questions.

For a while, I thought I'd been singled out for torment, which of course isn't true. Nobody knows why bad things happen to good people. The great thinkers of the world have made lifelong studies of the causes of human suffering, and they don't know why either. All of the world's religions grapple with this one perplexing truth: life is both joy *and* suffering. Life is a riddle, a mystery no one will ever fully understand.

Human beings are the most complex creatures on earth. On the one hand, we have created sophisticated organ transplant technology and genetic engineering, but we still know very little about spinal cord nerve damage.

I am certain that much of the reason I am walking today is because I desperately wanted to. And, I was prepared to do whatever was necessary to make it happen. I was fortunate not to have permanent spinal cord damage, but that doesn't negate what I've achieved. Some patients have given up with less damage than mine, simply because the will to persevere wasn't in them.

I truly believe that a person's will is what makes the difference between success and failure in all of life's challenges. I also believe in the power of the mind, in its ability to guide the healing powers of the body. So I did everything I could to train my mind to be my ally during the rehabilitation process.

I listened to audiotaped meditations by Dr. Bernie Siegel and read books by Dr. Joseph Murphy about the power of the subconscious mind. I listened constantly to the beautiful music of Enya, a gifted Irish composer. I used humor on myself and others. I did for my mind what the therapists were doing for my body—giving it exercise and discipline. I was visualizing myself getting well, seeing myself walk, and functioning as well as any other person in this society. But I know that I'm in a race that has no finish line.

My fall off a ladder changed my world and how I function in it. My life is the same, but different. I'm different. I've been blessed with adversity. I've learned to accept the limitations of my body. I know now it doesn't define who I am or what I can yet become. The Man in the Glass is much more focused now. I know where my strength comes from. It comes from deep inside, where there's a boy who used to play football in Brooklyn—that kid who grabbed hold of life and ran with it—that kid whom I'd forgotten about, until those slow and weary days I spent in the hospital.

Everyone's got a kid like that inside. It's the voice of possibility, of hope, of love. I see that kid reflected back to me in the eyes of my own children. I'm one hell of a lucky guy. I've been twice blessed.

EPILOGUE

Spinal cord injury, head injury, and stroke paralyze 842,000 Americans per year, 2,307 Americans per day, 97 Americans every hour, or one American every 37 seconds.

Paralysis need no longer be considered a lifetime prognosis. Indeed, with adequate funding, a targeted research program administered by a Science Advisory Council can lead to both the treatment of acute paralysis and the reversal of chronic paralysis.

Few investments could yield higher returns to society. Research on brain and spinal cord injury is not an option... it is a necessity. As diseases and sickness are conquered, injuries will dominate. Within our lifetime, injury to the central nervous system will become the major cause of disability for all people. Let us hope that we will understand it well enough to do something soon for the millions of people already paralyzed and the millions who will become victims.

Please do something now. Send your contribution to Kent Waldrep at the National Paralysis Foundation, 14651 Dallas Parkway, Suite 136, Dallas, Texas 75240, 214/387-CURE, to Project Support for Spinal Cord Injury, 11755 Wilshire Boulevard, Suite 860, Los Angeles, California 90025, 310/996-0311, or to The Challenge Center, 240 South Magnolia Avenue, El Cajon, California 92020, 619/588-5868.